Crayola Dream~Makers®

Building fun and creativity into standards-based learning

Mathematics

K through 6

Ron De Long, M.Ed.
Janet B. McCracken, M.Ed.
Elizabeth Willett, M.Ed.

A Hallmark Company

© 2009 Crayola, LLC
Easton, PA 18044-0431

Acknowledgements

This guide and the entire Crayola® Dream-Makers® series would not be possible without the expertise and tireless efforts of Ron De Long, Jan McCracken, and Elizabeth Willett. Your passion for children, the arts, and creativity are inspiring. Thank you. Special thanks also to Alison Panik for her content-area expertise, writing, research, and curriculum development of this guide.

Crayola also gratefully acknowledges the teachers and students who tested the lessons in this guide:

Barbi Bailey-Smith, Little River Elementary School, Durham, NC

Rob Bartoch, Sandy Plains Elementary School, Baltimore, MD

Susan Bivona, Mount Prospect Elementary School, Basking Ridge, NJ

Jennifer Braun, Oak Street Elementary School, Basking Ridge, NJ

Barbara Calvo, Ocean Township Elementary School, Oakhurst, NJ

Pat Check, Spring Garden Elementary School, Bethlehem, PA

Trish Davlante, Michael Jordan Community School, Chicago, IL

Regina DeFrancisco, Liberty Corner Elementary School, Basking Ridge, NJ

Beth Delaney, Fredon Township School, Newton, NJ

Carly Doughty, Little River Elementary School, Durham, NC

Amanda Warner Grantz, Oakhurst Elementary School, Fort Worth, TX

Barbara Grasso, John J. Jennings Elementary School, Bristol, CT

Craig Hinshaw, Hiller Elementary School, Madison Heights, MI

Janice House, Little River Elementary School, Durham, NC

Charlotte Ka, PS 132K, Brooklyn, NY

Nancy Knutsen, Triangle School, Hillsborough, NJ

Kay La Bella, Foothills Elementary School, Colorado Springs, CO

Kamyee Ladas, Mount Prospect Elementary School, Basking Ridge, NJ

Cara Lucente, Gayman Elementary School, Plumstead, PA

Jenna Makos, Catholic Charities After- School Program, Phillipsburg, NJ

Elyse Martin, Michael Jordan Community School, Chicago, IL

Annette Mauer, Freeman Elementary School, Phillipsburg, NJ

Marge Mayers, Barley Sheaf School, Flemington, NJ

Val Negra, Mountain Way Elementary School, Morris Plains, NJ

Jen O'Flaherty, Sandy Plains Elementary School, Baltimore, MD

Alison Panik, Trinity Kids Club, Trinity Wesleyan Church, Allentown, PA

Jennifer Parks, T. J. Lee Elementary School, Irving, TX

Kathy Prichard, Feeeman Elementary School, Phillipsburg, NJ

Nancy Rhoads, Curlew Creek Elementary School, Palm Harbor, FL

Lynn Schatzle, Wood Creek Elementary School, Farmington Hills, MI

Karen Sommerfeld, Foothills Elementary School, Colorado Springs, CO

Neila Steiner, CS 102, Bronx, NY

Tom Tschumper, Princeton North Elementary School, Princeton, MN

The language and concepts of mathematics and art are intrinsically linked, with both using symmetry, proportion, geometry, symbols, reasoning, linear perspective, and more. From Greek and Roman architects, to arts and inventors such as Leonardo do Vinci, Roy Lichtenstein, Kendall Shaw, and the Gee's Bend quilters, students explore our world, nature, and order in principles of art and design based on these concepts. We hope that these lessons will aid you in building children's creative problem-solving skills, and a deeper, memorable understanding of mathematics by experiencing and seeing these concepts through visual arts learning activities.

Nancy A. De Bellis
Director, Education Marketing
Crayola

Crayola Dream-Makers is a series of standards-based supplemental curriculum resources that contain lesson plans for educators teaching kindergarten through 6th grade. Each guide uses visual art lessons to stimulate critical thinking and problem-solving for individual subject areas such as Math, Language Arts, Science, and Social Studies. Students demonstrate and strengthen their knowledge while engaging in creative, fun, hands-on learning processes.

Table of Contents

Crayola **Dream~Makers**®
Building fun and creativity into standards-based learning

Each Crayola Dream-Makers guide provides elementary classroom and art teachers with 24 arts-focused lessons that extend children's learning and enhance academic skills. Align these lessons with your school district and state curriculum standards. Stay flexible in your teaching approaches with adaptations like these.

- **Be prepared.** Read through the lesson first. Create an art sample so you understand the process.
- **Discover new resources.** Each lesson contains background information, fine art and craft examples, representative student artwork, vocabulary builders, and discussion ideas. Use these suggestions as a springboard to find resources that address your students' interests and are pertinent to your community. Search Web sites such as Google Image to locate fine art. Stretch student imaginations and their awareness of the world around them.
- **Seek creative craft materials.** Ask children's families and local businesses to recycle clean, safe items for project use and take better care of the environment, too. *Recycle, Reuse, Renew!*
- **Showcase student achievements.** Create banners to accompany curriculum project displays in your class, school, or community. Post the lesson's standards-based objectives with displays to demonstrate broad-based student learning. Demonstrate how children's accomplishments have personal meaning and promote life-long learning through portfolio documentation.
- **Make this book your own.** Jot down your own ideas as you plan and reflect on students' learning experiences. Combine art techniques and lesson content to fit goals for your students and classroom. Substitute other transformative craft materials. With students, make content webs of possibilities for extending learning opportunities.
- **Build connections.** Collaborate with your students, other teachers, administrators, artists in residence, and community groups to plan lessons that are unique. Work together to promote creative thinking!
- **Write DREAM statements.** As part of the assessment process, students are asked to reflect on their work in a dream journal. Before the lesson, Dream statements are expected to capture children's prior knowledge about each topic. After each lesson, students state in writing how they will use what they have learned and dream about possibilities for future exploration.
- **Funding resources.** Crayola Dream-Makers lesson plans have been used in school programs funded by a variety of federal, state, local, and private grants. For more information about grants and grant writing visit The Foundation Center at www.fdncenter.org.

The lessons in this book are intended to address content benchmarks and grade-level expectations in mathematics along with a heavy concentration of key art concepts. All lessons are teacher- and student-tested and follow a consistent format to support you in planning creative, fun learning opportunities for your students.

Benefits of Arts Integration

The 2006 report *Critical Evidence–How the ARTS Benefit Student Achievement*, published by the National Assembly of State Arts Agencies in collaboration with the Arts Education Partnership, identifies a number of ways that arts learning experiences benefit students. Teachers who consciously integrate arts-based practice into their teaching bring these benefits to their students.

> "Certain arts activities promote growth in positive social skills, including self-confidence, self-control, conflict resolution, collaboration, empathy, and social tolerance. Research evidence demonstrates these benefits apply to all students, not just the gifted and talented. The arts can play a key role in developing social competencies among educationally or economically disadvantaged youth who are at greatest risk of not successfully completing their education." (p. 14)

According to Diane Watanabe and Richard Sjolseth, co-directors of the Institute of Learning, Teaching, and the Human Brain, when there is joy in learning, student achievement soars.

> "When students find joy in their creative outlets, there is a positive carryover to school in general. Emotion, interest, and motivation promote learning and memory. Brain research shows the brain produces at least three pleasure chemicals when joy is present: endorphins, dopamine, and serotonin. These chemicals account for the emotional states produced by self-satisfaction, positive self-image, passion for one's art, and joy in learning." (2006, p. 20)

Children learn in many different ways

Howard Gardner has identified eight types of intelligences and may add others. Arts-integrated learning experiences enable children to more fully develop a wide range of skills and understandings.

- **Linguistic intelligence** involves sensitivity to spoken and written language, the ability to learn languages, and the capacity to use language to accomplish certain goals.
- **Logical-mathematical intelligence** consists of the capacity to analyze problems logically, carry out mathematical operations, and investigate issues scientifically.
- **Musical intelligence** involves skill in the performance, composition, and appreciation of musical patterns.
- **Bodily-kinesthetic intelligence** entails the potential of using one's whole body or parts of the body to solve problems.
- **Spatial intelligence** involves the potential to recognize and use the patterns of wide space and more confined areas.
- **Interpersonal intelligence** is concerned with the capacity to understand the intentions, motivations, and desires of other people. It allows people to work effectively with others.
- **Intrapersonal intelligence** entails the capacity to understand oneself, to appreciate one's feelings, fears, and motivations.
- **Naturalist intelligence** enables human beings to recognize, categorize, and draw upon certain features of the environment. (Gardner, 1999: pp. 41-43, 52)

Find More Resources at www.crayola.com/educators

Supplementary materials for Dream-Makers guides include:

- Printable certificates for recognizing children's participation and adults' support
- Thousands of images of children's art
- Demonstration videos for teaching arts-integrated lessons
- Printable resource guides for educators and administrators
- More than 1,000 free, cross-curricular lesson plan ideas on wide-ranging topics, all developed by experienced educators. Sign up for free monthly newsletters to keep you abreast of the newest Crayola products, events, and projects.

Bibliography

Gardner, H. (1999). *Intelligence Reframed: Multiple Intelligences for the 21st Century.* New York: Basic Books.

Marzano, R.J. (March 2005). *ASCD Report–Preliminary Report on the 2004-05 Evaluation Study of the ASCD Program for Building Academic Vocabulary.* Reston, VA: Association for Supervision and Curriculum Development.

National Assembly of State Arts Agencies (NASAA) in collaboration with the Arts Education Partnership. (2006). *Critical Evidence–How the ARTS Benefit Student Achievement.* Washington, DC: Author.

Smith, M.K. (2002). Howard Gardner and multiple intelligences. The encyclopedia of informal education, http://www.infed.org/thinkers/gardner.htm. Retrieved from http://www.infed.org/thinkers/gardner.htm May 9, 2007. Reprinted with permission.

Watanabe, D., & Sjolseth, R. (2006). *Lifetime Payoffs: The Positive Effect of the Arts on Human Brain Development.* Miami, FL: NFAA youngARTS. Reprinted with permission.

Garden of Colorful Counting

Objectives

Students recognize sets of objects and understand numbers and ways of representing them.

Children create and count beds of garden flowers in colorful collages to demonstrate that they understand sets and their representations.

Multiple Intelligences

| Logical-mathematical | Spatial |
| Naturalist | |

National Standards

Visual Arts Standard #3	Mathematics Standards
Chooses and evaluates a range of subject matter, symbols, and ideas	**Number and Operations** Understand numbers, ways of representing numbers, relationships among numbers, and number systems Understand meanings of operations and how they relate to one another Compute fluently and make reasonable estimates **Problem Solving** Build new mathematical knowledge through problem solving Solve problems that arise in mathematics and in other context Apply and adapt a variety of appropriate strategies to solve problems Monitor and reflect on the process of mathematical problem solving

Background Information

In April 1887 a spectacular marvel occurred. A shipment of 20 glass flowers arrived in New York City from Dresden, Germany. The flowers were the first of 847 life-size glass models that were created and shipped to Harvard University in Cambridge, Massachusetts. Two German artists, Leopold Blaschka and his son Rudolf, created these garden marvels that included models of plants, flowers, and other botanical specimens.

Today the more than 3,000 glass flowers and plants are used mostly as teaching tools for students studying the plant sciences at Harvard. In addition to being stunningly accurate to the smallest detail, these spectacular wonders are in bloom all year. The Ware Collection of Glass Models of Plants, as the collection is known, is housed in two rooms on the third floor of the Botanical Museum of Harvard University. It is the only collection of its kind in the world.

Resources

Alison's Zinnia by Anita Lobel
Dazzling display of botanically correct illustrations arranged in an alphabet book format. Collection of detailed flowers of various colors, shapes, and sizes.

Planting a Rainbow by Lois Ehlert
Colorful collage-style illustrations. Inspires children and adults alike to plant gardens of blooms both in soil and on paper. Rich language and high-quality artwork supplement early elementary studies of plants, flowers, color, and counting.

Rooster's Off to See the World by Eric Carle
Rooster collects—and counts—companions along his travels. Carle's colorful collages lead early elementary children through an addition and subtraction adventure of counting up and counting down.

The Glass Flowers at Harvard by Richard Evans Schultes and William A. Davis
For upper-elementary and middle school students. Photo essay presents Harvard's unique collection of amazing glass flowers and the story of how they were made.

Vocabulary List

Use this list to explore new vocabulary, create idea webs, or brainstorm related subjects.

- Math concepts

Classify	Fraction	Organize
Collection	Group	Pair
Compare	Less	Percentage
Decimal	More	Set
Dozen	Number	Skip counting
Equal	Numeral	Sort
Even	Odd	

- Art concepts

Collage	Rubbing	Texture

- Science concepts

Bulb	Petal	Stamen
Flower	Pistil	Stem
Leaf	Seed	

Floral Motif Textile from Kashmir, India
Contemporary, date unknown
Artisan unknown
Private Collection.

Artwork by students from St. Theresa School,
Hellertown, Pennsylvania.

Artwork by students from
Little River Elementary School,
Durham, North Carolina.
Teachers: Barbi Bailey-Smith,
Carly Doughty, Janice House

Monet's Garden
Photo by R. De Long

Crayola Dream~Makers®
Building fun and creativity into standards-based learning

Garden of Colorful Counting

	K-2	3-4	5-6
Suggested Preparation and Discussion	Show three flowers in a plastic vase and two others loose. Guide children to create number sentences identifying how many flowers they count in total and how many are in the sets in and out of the vase. Arrange different sets in the vase to practice this skill. Collect visual examples of different types of flowers, both real and in photographs and other art. Display pictures of flower gardens and gardens with multiple beds of plants. Read the book *Rooster's Off to See the World* aloud. Stop at various points in the story to ask questions such as, "If we had two small sheds, how many animals could we put in each shed?" Invite children to explain how they would group the animals.	Show a box with three clay pots inside and two outside. Ask children to write math sentences identifying how many clay pots they count in total, and how many are in sets inside and outside the box. Try different combinations of same size sets in and out of the box. Encourage the use of multiplication. Display a bouquet of flowers and books of flowers for children to look at and use to make flower sketches. Invite children to choose which flowers are their personal favorites and explore why. Is it the color, size, shape, fragrance, design of the flower, or some other attribute that appeals to them?	Show a garden diagram with four equal sections, each section labeled with a different type of flower. Ask students to create mathematical statements about this garden using fraction, decimal, and percentage computations. Change the diagram to offer different computation opportunities. Display a variety of examples of flowers, real ones, books, and catalogs about flowers, and art depicting flowers. Invite students to explore these resources to prepare to design their own garden plots.
Crayola® Supplies	• Crayons • School Glue • Scissors		
Other Materials	• Construction paper • Plastic bags that seal • Tag board, poster board, or recycled file folders • Textured materials such as leaves, plastic sink mats, very coarse sandpaper, screens, netting, or latch-hook mats		• Rolled craft paper
Set-up/Tips	• Cover any sharp edges on textured materials (such as screens) with thick layers of masking tape. • Students label plastic bags with their names.		
Process: Session 1 20-30 min.	**Create sets** 1. Students put a variety of objects into sets, such as crayons, desks, and people. 2. Students justify why they created the sets. Combine sets and record the findings.	**Use multiples and division** 1. Students show multiplication and division of sets of objects with concrete models such as marbles or books to achieve multiplication facts such as 2 x 3 = 6. 2. Students demonstrate correct results.	**Use equivalent fractions** 1. Students show equivalent fractions with concrete models. Use cut shapes to experiment. 2. Create a number representation of the model for equivalent fractions such as 1/4 + 1/4 + 1/4 + 1/4 = 1; 2/8 + 4/16 + 1/2 = 1. 3. Challenge students to demonstrate a proof.
Process: Session 2 20-30 min.	**Create texture rubbings** 3. Place construction paper on top of flat textured materials. Rub over the paper with the side of an unwrapped crayon. Press hard to achieve dramatic color effects. Encourage children to experiment.		
		Create blended-color rubbings 3. For unique multicolor effects, rub two different colors over the same texture.	**Create shadow rubbing effects** 4. Experiment with different effects: Move the paper slightly and rub a second time with a different color. Or rub over a different textured item.

	K-2	3-4	5-6
Process: Session 3 20-30 min.	**Create flowers** 5. Cut simple, small flower shapes from the textured rubbing papers. Create multiples of several kinds of flowers. Make some flowers unique. Create new species of flowers that are not known to science. Add stems and leaves to the flowers. Store flowers in plastic bags.		
Process: Session 4 20-30 min.	**Build a set garden** 6. On paper, students write number phrases such as 3 + 4 + 2. 7. Fold another sheet of paper in half. Along the fold draw a garden divider, such as a fence post, scarecrow, or birdhouse, to separate two garden beds. 8. Glue flowers into place to show the number phrases. Air-dry the glue.	**Build a multiplication garden** 6. On paper, students write a multiplication fact. 7. Glue flowers grouped in sets inside beds to reflect the multiplication fact. 8. Use crayons to outline blossoms. Draw flower features such as stems and leaves. Add other garden objects to each bed.	**Build an equivalent fraction garden** 6. On paper, students write an equivalent fraction fact. 7. Teams of students glue flower groupings reflecting equivalent fraction facts on craft paper to create a garden mural.
Assessment	• Children count the number of flowers they drew in both beds and write the numerals on their drawings or on a separate paper. • Children write math sentences describing the flowers in their collages in different ways. Check for accuracy.	• Children write math sentences describing the flowers in their collages in different ways. Encourage them to try to write addition, subtraction, multiplication, and division sentences. Check for accuracy.	• Students write mathematical descriptions of their garden plans. Ask them to use fraction, decimal, and percentage terms to describe the ways they could plant different flowers in their gardens. Interview students as needed.
	• Ask students to reflect on this lesson and write a DREAM statement to summarize the most important things they learned.		
Extensions	Children create a collage depicting a garden. Display gardens in pairs on a bulletin board with a strip of paper (fence) separating each pair. Invite children to count and compare the number of flowers of different types (colors, sizes, shapes) in each pair of gardens. Plant mini gardens. Fill recycled containers with soil. Use craft sticks to divide each mini garden into two beds. Plant seeds in each bed. Record number of seeds planted. As plants grow, continue to record the number of seedlings on each half, the number of leaves, flowers, and other details. Sketch the plants' progress. Keep excitement for gardens growing! Check out the Underground Garden lesson plan on Crayola.com!	Students design their own gardens with colored pencils, stamps, rulers, and markers. Encourage students to choose their favorite flowers and calculate percentages, fractions, and decimal descriptions of the use of space in their virtual gardens. Calculate perimeter and area. Fence in the garden with toothpicks. Plan, plot, and plant flower gardens in a schoolyard, community park, or at a local retirement community. Solicit flower donations from local nurseries and businesses. Use math skills to plan and calculate how flower beds will be divided and filled with color. Visit the garden, photograph the beds, and use math to describe the results. Take a different view of flowers with lesson plans such as Table for Two or Fluttering Focus on Crayola.com.	

Objectives

Children identify geometric shapes and differentiate the attributes of symmetry and asymmetry in a variety of different shapes.

Children in grades 3 to 6 research their facial images with mirrors to prove symmetry or asymmetry.

Children in grades 5-6 sculpt a symmetrical 3-D model of their 2-D drawing.

Children design a face whose details demonstrate symmetry.

Multiple Intelligences

Logical-mathematical
Naturalist
Spatial

What Does It Mean?

Asymmetry: when one side of a point, line, or plane is arranged so that it differs from and does not balance with the opposite side

Bas-relief: short 3-D projections on a surface, as in sculpture or weaving

Symmetry: when one side of a point, line, or plane balances another, with opposite sides demonstrating identical or similar arrangement, form, and size

National Standards

Visual Arts Standard #2
Uses knowledge of structures and functions

Mathematics Standards
Geometry
Apply transformations and use symmetry to analyze mathematical situations
Grades 3-6
Reasoning and Proof
Select and use various types of reasoning and methods of proof

Background Information

Alexander Calder, "Sandy" to his friends, was born near Philadelphia, Pennsylvania, to a family of artists. When Sandy was only 5 years old, he made little wood and wire people and animals. At age 8, he made jewelry for his sister Peggy's doll. Sandy always liked to think of new contraptions. In the fourth grade he made an ink-blotting pad to hang on the side of his desk. As an adult he invented many new and playful ways to make sculpture, including portraits out of wire; hanging, moving mobiles; and giant standing steel stabiles. Many of the shapes observed in this art illustrate asymmetry.

Joan Miró was born in 1893 in Barcelona, Spain, in a region known as Catalonia. He began to make art at the age of 8. As a young man, a serious illness ended his career as a bookkeeper and contributed to his decision to dedicate himself to painting. Like other artists of the early 20th century, he was drawn to Paris, France, where he met many other important artists. His art is marked by his use of expressive colors, lines, and large shapes, often arranged on a simple background, conveying a dreamlike atmosphere. Miró always stayed close to his Catalan roots, and often incorporated the people, places, and folk art images of his native land in his work. Like Calder, many of the shapes observed in Miró's art depict asymmetry.

Resources

It Looked Like Spilt Milk by Charles G. Shaw
Splotches of spilt milk against a blue background inspire all ages to envision other images such as a rabbit, a squirrel, or a tree. Illustrations lead students to see the world in a new way.

The Essential Alexander Calder by Howard Greenfield
Hanging, dangling, harmoniously asymmetrical mobiles accompany an account of Calder's life. Fascinating facts, compelling quotes, and background about cultural influences appeal to upper elementary students.

When Pigasso Met Mootisse by Nina Laden
Feuding animal artists turn their neighboring farms into dueling works of art. Bold colors, contrasting portrait and painting styles, and clever humor appeal to students in all grades. Provides details about the parodied artists, Picasso and Matisse.

Concept List

Use this list to explore new vocabulary, create idea webs, or brainstorm related subjects.

• Natural symmetry	Animals & insects Human faces	Leaves
• Symmetry in the arts	Performing arts Dance Mime	Visual arts Architecture Oriental and Persian rugs Pottery
• Explore symmetry	Capital letters Palindromes Reflection & mirror image	Symmetrical plane figures
• Terms	Assymetry Balance Bilateral symmetry Congruence Line of symmetry Near symmetry Radial symmetry	Symmetrical balance Symmetry Three dimensional Two dimensional

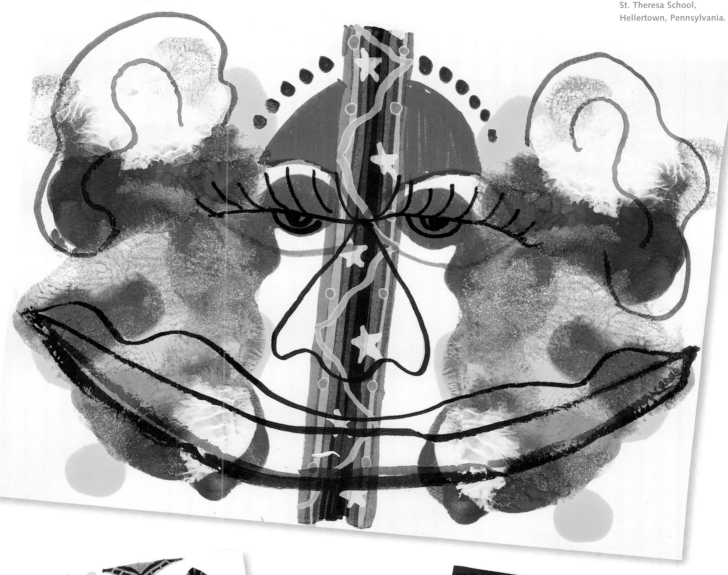

Artwork by students from
St. Theresa School,
Hellertown, Pennsylvania.

Artwork by students
from Catholic Charities
After-School Program,
Phillipsburg, New Jersey.
Teacher: Jenna Makos

Artwork by students from
Foothills Elementary School,
Colorado Springs, Colorado.
Teachers: Kay La Bella,
Karen Sommerfeld

Crayola **Dream~Makers**®
Building fun and creativity into standards-based learning

In the Face of Symmetry

	K-2	3-4	5-6
Suggested Preparation and Discussion	Ask children to name basic shapes. List all the shapes children can find in the classroom. Read *It Looked Like Spilt Milk* or a similar title. Children cut or tear assorted colored paper shapes. Imagine what the shapes could be. Draw lines or fold down the middle of shapes to illustrate symmetry and asymmetry.	Review symmetry. Challenge students to identify which English capital letters are symmetrical. Explore symmetry in the human face and nature. Use mirrors to review and explore the concept. Fold magazine pictures of face in half and place fold against mirror to see symmetry of the full face. Are all faces symmetrical or near symmetrical? Take a digital photograph of each student's full face. Print each photo on copy paper. Fold sheets in half on the face's line of symmetry and place fold against a mirror to compare symmetrical face with actual face.	Discuss that a line of symmetry can exist in two AND three dimensions. Think of examples. The human face appears flat in photographs but really it is a three dimensional (3-D) object. It has height, width, and depth. 3-D objects can be represented with 2-D symbols but 3-D objects are quite different. A circle can represent a sphere. A square a cube, a triangle a pyramid, a rectangle a rectangular prism.
	Look at reproductions of art created by Joan Miró and Alexander Calder. Display portraits by Matisse and Picasso. Read *When Pigasso Met Mootisse* or another appropriate book. Talk about how symmetry and asymmetry affect the balance of shapes and features.		
Crayola® Supplies	• Markers • Overwriters® Markers • Paint • Paint Brushes		• Colored Pencils • Markers • Model Magic® • School Glue
Other Materials	• Paper towels • Recycled newspaper • Water containers • White drawing paper		• Tag board • White paper
Set-up/Tips	• Cover painting surface with recycled newspaper. • Encourage children to load brush so they have enough paint to make substantial shapes, but not so much that strokes are hard to control.		• Draw first half of face on one side of paper using heavy pencil marks. Fold paper in half and hold to window. Trace other half of drawing on opposite side of paper.
Process: Session 1 20-30 min.	**Paint shapes and fold** 1. Fold paper in half. Crease. Open paper flat. 2. Use an Overwriters Under-Color Marker to draw a line along the fold. 3. Paint a variety of shapes on **one side** of the fold. 4. While the paint is still wet, fold paper closed. Press down gently with palm and fingers. Be careful not to push paint beyond the edges of the paper. 5. Open the paper. Are painted designs on both sides of the paper symmetrical or asymmetrical? Air-dry painted designs.		**Draw symmetrical monster face** 1. Fold paper in half. Crease. Open flat. 2. Draw one half of monster face using geometric shapes on one side of the fold. 3. Fold drawing back to opposite side of paper. 4. Hold up the drawing to a window and trace the drawing on the opposite side of the page. Open to reveal a complete symmetrical face.

Polish Paper Cuttings
Artist unknown
Cut colored paper
9" x 9"
Private Collection.

	K-2	3-4	5-6
Process: Session 2 20-30 min.	**Find a face and add details** 6. Study positions of painted shapes. Search for a face among the shapes. 7. Fill areas around the face shape with Overwriters Under-Color Markers to bring out facial features. Outline shapes with lines of color. 8. Embellish and strengthen the face concept by adding details with both Under- and Over-Color Markers.		**Add details** 5. Add additional symmetrical details if necessary. 6. Add color to the various shapes of the face keeping consistent with the idea of symmetry.
Process: Session 3 15-20 min.		**Research symmetry and near symmetry** 9. Position artwork with line of symmetry along a mirror to reveal whether it is perfect symmetry. Compare reflection with actual artwork. 10. Slide mirrors across artwork to see new symmetrical faces and designs.	**Create a 3-D model** 7. Using the 2-D plan as a guide, create a 3-D model of the monster face with Model Magic compound on tag board. Determine the line of symmetry. 8. Create 3-D forms, such as spheres where circles were used in 2-D. Glue pieces in place. 9. Add symmetrical details with markers. 10. Display 2-D drawings with 3-D models and objectives.
Assessment	• Children identify shapes in their own artwork and the artwork of classmates. • Children explain the details that make their face designs symmetrical.	• Older children draw faces with increasing levels of detail. • Students explain how their own artwork is symmetrical in a written or oral proof, citing evidence proving the symmetrical features in the faces they created. • Students recognize where plan modifications were necessary for completion of the project. • Students identify details that create asymmetry in each other's artwork.	
			• Students correctly represented 2-D shapes with 3-D forms to sculpt a bas-relief model of their plans.
	• Ask students to reflect on this lesson and write a DREAM statement to summarize the most important things they learned.		
Extensions	Make symmetrical cloud books. Children paint several symmetrical cloud shapes on small squares of blue paper. Attach dry cloud designs to every other page of a folded paper book. Children write or draw about what they see in each design. Younger children and those with visual or visual processing impairments may find it helpful to trace the dried paint shapes with their fingers, one on each side.	Students make symmetrical names. Print first names using all capital letters. Identify letters that are symmetrical. Draw lines of symmetry through each symmetrical letter. Next fold colored paper (one piece for each letter), crease, and open flat. Paint one half of each symmetrical letter along the fold and press closed. Open. Paint asymmetrical letters on one side of the fold line, being sure one edge of the letter is on the fold. Press paper closed. Open to reveal the new letter design. Air-dry all letters. Cut out letters and glue names on colored poster board. Expand symmetry research into the third dimension with the Sweet Symmetry craft on Crayola.com. Encourage children with exceptional talents to identify symmetry in a variety of art forms, letters or characters in other languages, vehicle design, and other challenging topics.	
	Let symmetry studies take flight with the Insect Symmetry lesson plan on Crayola.com.		

Gee's-ometric Wisdom

Objectives

Students identify increasingly advanced geometric shapes and demonstrate how several shapes can be combined to create new and different shapes.

Students experiment with various geometric designs to create aesthetically pleasing paper quilts using their own original patterned papers.

Children use the language of mathematics appropriate to their grade and ability levels to write and talk about geometric relationships in quilt designs created by themselves and their classmates.

Multiple Intelligences

| Linguistic |
| Logical-mathematical |
| Spatial |

What Does It Mean?

Balance: equal distribution of colors, lines, textures, and shapes to give parts of a composition equal visual weight or emphasis

Congruence: the harmonious relationship between figures that are the same size and the same shape

Symmetry: when one side of a point, line, or plane balances another with opposite sides demonstrating identical or similar arrangement, form, and size

National Standards

Visual Arts Standard #4 Understanding the visual arts in relation to history and cultures **Visual Arts Standard #6** Making connections between visual arts and other disciplines	**Mathematics Standards** *Geometry* Use visualization, spatial reasoning, and geometric modeling to solve problems *Communication* Communicate their mathematical thinking coherently and clearly to peers, teachers, and others

Background Information

People create quilts to keep themselves covered and warm. Quilts can also be objects of beauty. The women of Gee's Bend—a small, remote community in rural Alabama—have created hundreds of quilt masterpieces for about 100 years. They traditionally work with used, discarded, or rejected bits of cloth and follow linear patterns that combine shape and color, often with the flavor of the African textile traditions handed down from their ancestors. Gee's Bend (and many other) quilts are products of everyday life, mental agility, deep sensitivity, and geometric genius. Gee's Bend quilts are even featured on U.S. postage stamps!

Resources

Shapes, Shapes, Shapes by Tana Hoban
Wordless picture book. Challenges young students to find geometric shapes in everyday life. Shapes include circles, parallelograms, triangles, and stars.

The Quilts of Gee's Bend by John Beardsley, William Arnett, Pauljane Arnett, & Jan Livingston
Older elementary students enjoy these stories of the lives of the quilters of Gee's Bend, Alabama. Illustrated with color photographs of the geometric quilts made by these women.

The Rag Coat by Lauren A. Mills
Readers learn that patterned fabric scraps are more than just the sum of their shapes, sizes, and colors. Touching story for all ages.

Vocabulary List

Use this list to explore new vocabulary, create idea webs, or brainstorm related subjects.

- Geometric terms

Circle	Perpendicular
Congruence	Rectangle
Hexagon	Square
Octagon	Symmetry
Parallel	Triangle
Parallelogram	

- Visual arts vocabulary

Arrangement	Light
Balance	Pattern
Border	Quilting designs
Contrast	Grandmother's
Design	Flower Garden
Hue	Log Cabin
Illusion	Wedding Ring
Juxtaposition	Quilting frame
	Shadow

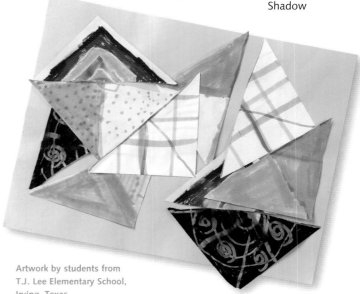

Artwork by students from
T.J. Lee Elementary School,
Irving, Texas.
Teacher: Jennifer Parks

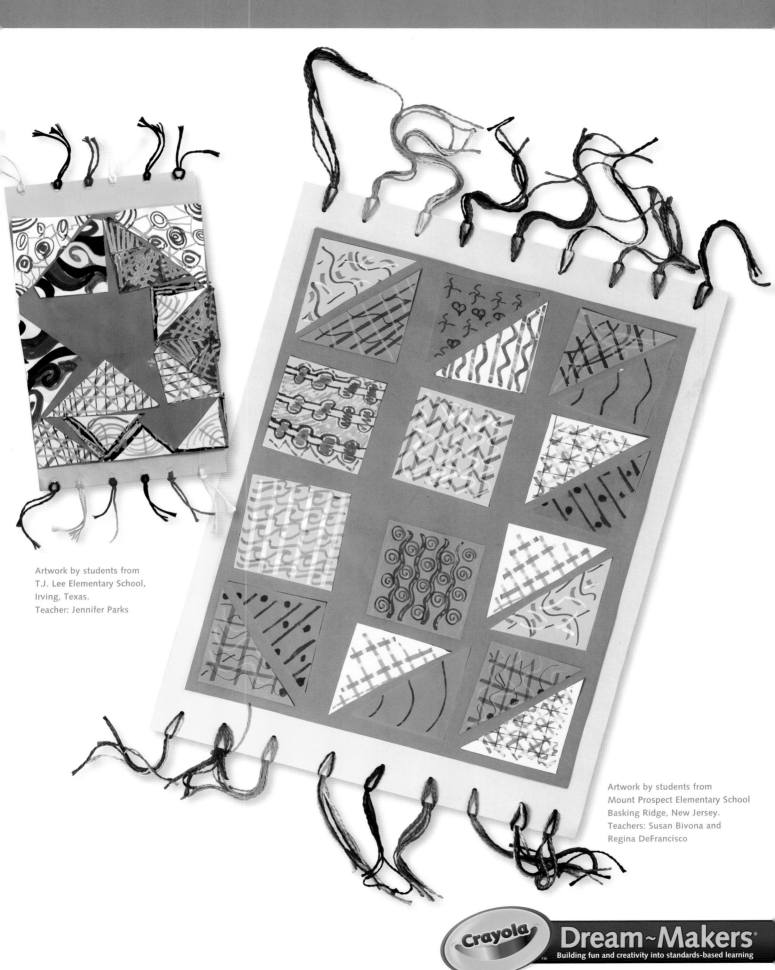

Artwork by students from
T.J. Lee Elementary School,
Irving, Texas.
Teacher: Jennifer Parks

Artwork by students from
Mount Prospect Elementary School
Basking Ridge, New Jersey.
Teachers: Susan Bivona and
Regina DeFrancisco

Crayola **Dream~Makers**®
Building fun and creativity into standards-based learning

Gee's-ometric Wisdom

	K-2	3-4	5-6
Suggested Preparation and Discussion	With students, prepare a display of quilts or quilt pictures. Show shapes such as rectangles, squares, triangles, circles, parallelograms, and a rhombus near the quilt display.		
	Invite students to identify basic geometric shapes in their environments. Experiment with how paper shapes can be combined to make new shapes. Who can put two triangles together to form a square? What shape is formed when several squares are set side by side? Demonstrate how cutting one shape can transform it into others.	Review increasingly more complicated geometric shapes. Introduce vocabulary of geometric relationships such as angles, symmetry, adjacent, parallel, perpendicular, and congruent. Demonstrate the illusionary effects of juxtaposing light and dark contrasting shapes. Research several sophisticated quilt designs. Identify all of the shapes used. How are the shapes oriented to create the designs? How does the quilt design demonstrate balance and symmetry? Can students find congruent shapes within the quilt designs? Ask students to find and describe examples of shapes within shapes.	
	Examine and discuss quilt display. What connections can students make between geometry and quilt design?		
			Discuss number concepts including multiplication fact families, fractions, decimals, percentages. How could these concepts be represented visually? Brainstorm and illustrate examples.
Crayola® Supplies	• Colored Pencils • Markers • School Glue • Scissors		
Other Materials	• Construction paper • Hole punch • Ruler • Sealable plastic bags • Yarn		
Set-up/Tips	• Store papers between sessions in labeled, sealable plastic bags.		
Process: Session 1 15-20 min.	**Design paper** 1. Children measure and cut at least four 4-inch paper squares and one 9-inch square. 2. Fill the small squares with decorative lines, shapes, and patterns in a variety of contrasting hues.		**Prepare quilt squares** 1. Children measure and cut at least six 6-inch paper quilt squares and one mounting paper large enough to hold all the paper squares without overlapping. 2. Select a math concept to represent. Draw the concept a different way in each quilt square.

Detail of quilt pattern illustrates how geometric shapes are pieced together to create a pattern.

Quilt, Circa 1965, by Mary L. Bennett of Gee's Bend, Alabama.
Cotton and cotton/polyester blend. 77" x 82"
Reproduced by permission of Tinwood Ventures.

Quilt, circa 1955, by Sue Willie Seltzer of Gee's Bend, Alabama.
Cotton and synthetic blends. 80" x 76"
Reproduced by permission of Tinwood Ventures.

	K-2	3-4	5-6
Process: Session 2 20-30 min.	**Cut triangles** 3. Fold a square diagonally, then open flat. Cut along fold line to create two triangles. Fold a few triangles in half and cut along folds to create smaller triangles.		**Color patterns** 3. Plan color for the concept. Make sure color patterns support the concept and add to design effectiveness. 4. Fill the patterns with color.
	Create more triangles 4. Cut other squares into a variety of triangle sizes and shapes.	**Create additional shapes** 4. Fold some squares in other directions. Cut shapes such as smaller squares, rectangles, and parallelograms. Encourage students to make a variety of shapes.	
Process: Session 3 20-30 min.	**Design with triangles** 5. Children arrange triangles on the 9-inch paper to form new decorative squares.	**Design with shapes** 5. Students experiment with various arrangements of shapes on the 9-inch paper to create new patterns and designs.	5. Experiment with various arrangements of quilt squares on mounting paper.

6. Encourage children to rotate, slide, and reposition shapes to see various effects. Invite them to look at each other's arrangements and exchange ideas. Settle on a final design. Glue shapes on the paper.

7. Mount square to a larger sheet in a contrasting color.

8. Punch several holes across top and bottom borders of mounting paper. Tie yarn through holes.

| **Process Session 4 20-30 min.** | 9. Children orally explain their design decisions using geometric and visual arts terms. 10. Students write one or two sentences describing the project. Display projects and colorful sentences together. | 9. Students write paragraphs describing the mathematical thinking used in designing their projects. How did they decide which shapes to combine? What were the results? What revisions did they make and why? Encourage use of mathematical terms. Display projects and colorful paragraphs together. 10. Invite students to orally compare and contrast their projects. What similarities and differences do they notice? What are some particularly effective designs? Why? | |

Assessment

• Are students able to recognize and identify increasingly more sophisticated geometric shapes within each other's quilt designs? Can older students identify elements that show balance, symmetry, and congruence? Do patterned papers include an ever-increasing variety of colors and designs?

• Do projects reflect an understanding of overall math concepts? Do projects reflect an understanding of how different shapes can be combined to form new shapes? Do project designs reflect a complexity commensurate with the ages and abilities of the students who created them? Did students in grades 3 to 6 use a variety of shapes in their designs? Did students in grades 5 and 6 identify and accurately represent concepts in their quilt designs?

• Do students use appropriately precise vocabulary in describing their design procedures orally and/or in writing?

• Ask students to reflect on this lesson and write a DREAM statement to summarize the most important things they learned.

Extensions

Create a class quilt with Crayola Fabric Crayons or Fabric Markers. Use design concepts learned from the paper quilt project. Ask parents to iron students' patterns on fabric squares. Recruit a community volunteer to sew fabric squares together. Display quilt and/or donate it to a local charity.

Invite students with an interest in research to investigate and present quilting traditions of various cultures. Discuss similarities and differences.

Invite a local quilter to show quilt samples and demonstrate design and sewing techniques.

Check out quilt-related lesson plans on Crayola.com such as Patchwork Quilt Lesson and Amish Quilters.

Provide colorful wooden pattern blocks for students who learn best from kinesthetic exercises.

Patterns of Love Beads

Objectives

Children sculpt three-dimensional geometric beads for 1960s hippie-style necklaces.

Students compare and order their formed beads in various color, shape, and sizes to represent patterns (grades K-2), multiplication (grades 3-4), and algebraic equations (grades 5-6).

Multiple Intelligences

Interpersonal
Logical-mathematical
Musical
Spatial

What Does It Mean?

Marbleize: knead at least two colors a little to achieve a marble effect

Pattern: orderly, repeated designs

National Standards

Visual Arts Standard #1	Mathematics Standards
Understands and applies media, techniques, and processes	**Algebra** (Grades K-6) Understand patterns, relations, and functions **Geometry** (Grades K-6) Use visualization, spatial reasoning, and geometric modeling to solve problems **Connections** (Grades K-6) Recognize and apply mathematics in contexts outside of mathematics **Number and Operations** (Grades 3-4) Understand numbers, ways of representing numbers, relationships among numbers, and number systems

Background Information

Beads have been made and used by humans for a variety of purposes for centuries. In an article in *Lapidary Journal*, Lynda McDaniel wrote, "Beads were among humans' earliest expression of abstract ideas. Although not functional in the sense of a tool or a weapon, beads carry strong symbolic significance."

In the late 1960s, young people used necklaces of "love beads" to show their rejection of violence and their hopes for peace, reflecting the mood of the times. Although both men and women wear necklaces today, in the 1960s young men who wore love beads were making a social statement of protest against war and expressing their desire for universal fellowship. These necklaces were often hand-made and exchanged as signs of love and friendship.

Resources

A String of Beads by Margarette S. Reade
Picture book for early elementary students. Beads are celebrated as little pieces of the world with stories to tell. Cheerful story presents facts about the history of beads and beading.

Beads of the World by Peter Francis, Jr.
Atlas of colorful photographs of hundreds of beads, with origins and uses. Younger students enjoy the photographs. Descriptions pique interest in world cultures for older students.

The Storyteller's Beads by Jane Kurtz
Based on personal accounts of Ethiopian refugees in the 1980s. Upper-elementary novel presents the stories of two refugee girls on a pilgrimage to Sudan. One girl relies on her grandmother's beads to remind her of the many stories of her ancestors' bravery.

Vocabulary List

Use this list to explore new vocabulary, create idea webs, or brainstorm related subjects.

- Pattern concepts

Concrete objects	Pairs	Sequence
Form	Prediction	Sets
Movement	Problem-solving	Skip-counting
Music	Relationships	Tables
Numbers	Repetition	

- Multiplication concepts

Equivalent sets	Fact families	Factors

- Algebra concepts

Cause and effect	Integers	Variables

- Geometry concepts

Congruence	Space figures	Space figures (contd.)
Similarity	Cone	Rectangular prism
Size	Cube	Sphere
	Cylinder	Triangular prism
	Elongated sphere	

- Bead concepts

History	Materials	Techniques
Decoration	Clay	Baking
Socialization	Glass	Carving
Storytelling	Seed	Firing
Trade	Stone	Stringing
Worship	Wood	

Math bead pattern necklaces
A. Multiplication—8x4
B. Reflective Symmetry
C. Red Bead Forms—Pyramid, Cone, Cube, Sphere, Cylinder
D. Fractions—1/8, 1/4, 1/2, 1, 1/2, 1/4, 1/8

Artwork by students from
Spring Garden Elementary School,
Bethlehem, Pennsylvania.
Teacher: Pat Check

Czech Molded Bead Necklace
Artist unknown
24"
Monofilament and glass
Private Collection.

Patterns of Love Beads

	K-2	3-4	5-6
Suggested Preparation and Discussion	Define the word *pattern* by showing examples. Ask children to find patterns in their everyday lives, such as clothing, calendars, and seasons. Refer to concrete examples whenever possible. Make a list of places where children see, hear, or experience patterns.	Display one or two plastic bead necklaces demonstrating multiples of one number (3 red, 3 blue, 3 yellow). String others that demonstrate more complex multiples (2 green, 3 purple, 2 green, 3 purple). Have corresponding math flashcards on hand. Challenge students to match flashcards with necklaces. Ask students to figure out how bead patterns and multiplication are related.	Create an assortment of plastic bead necklaces demonstrating algebraic equations. Choose statements such as these: $2(2a + 3b + 4c)$ $3(5x + 2y)$ $7(a + b + 2c)$ where different bead colors, shapes, or sizes represent variables. Challenge children to identify the equations in bead patterns.

Discuss the ways artists use patterns and repetition in their art as they repeat designs, colors, and figures. A good example of the use of patterns in art is the bead necklaces, called hippie or love beads, worn in the 1960s. Display images or reproductions of hippie-era bead necklaces with patterns. Invite children to share observations about patterns they see.

Make a sample bead necklace to show students. Use colored Crayola Model Magic® compound to form several marble-size geometric figures. String the beads in patterns of figures and colors.

Crayola® Supplies

- Colored Pencils
- Markers
- Model Magic®
- Scissors

Other Materials

- Clear adhesive tape
- Cotton cord or heavy string
- Modeling tools
- Paper plates
- Plastic drinking straws
- Pony beads (available at most craft stores)

Set-up/Tips

- Children help cut drinking straws into 1-inch (2 cm) pieces so they extend beyond the ends of the modeled beads. Each student will use about 20 pieces. Trim straws with scissors after beads dry.
- Mix white Model Magic compound with color from washable markers to make new hues.
- To create marbled beads, combine small amounts of two or three Model Magic colors. Knead and twist modeling compound with fingers for desired marble effect.
- For longer necklaces, use pony beads to separate Model Magic beads or bead pattern segments.
- Work and air-dry beads on paper plates labeled with children's names.
- Seal string ends with tape so children can wear beads. Close adult supervision is essential whenever children wear anything around their necks.

Round Ceramic Glazed Beads
Artist unknown
Glass and string
20"
Private Collection.

Turquoise Seed Bead Necklace
Artist unknown
Turquoise and horn clasp
26"
Private Collection.

Powder Glass
Beaded Necklace
Artist unknown
Glass and cotton threads
30"
Private Collection.

	K-2	3-4	5-6
Process: Session 1 20-30 min.	**Plan simple patterns** 1. Sketch necklace patterns. Plan the colors and shapes that will repeat to form patterns. 2. Children work in pairs to check each other's design patterns. 3. Demonstrate how to chant a pattern: "Red, blue, yellow! Red, blue, yellow!" as a way to feel the pattern's rhythm.	**Plan multiplication patterns** 1. Students choose multiplication facts to demonstrate in their necklace designs. 2. Draw plans for the use of shape, size, and color to show the math facts in bead patterns. 3. Trade bead pattern plans with partners. Challenge partners to identify the math fact in the pattern plan.	**Plan algebraic patterns** 1. Students write algebraic equations describing the necklace patterns they plan to create. 2. Draw necklace design plans using color, shape, and/or size as the variables of the algebraic equations. 3. Partners check each other's bead design plans to be sure they represent the algebraic equations accurately.

Process: Session 2 30-40 min.

Create beads

4. Select a marble-size amount of Model Magic compound for each bead. Add marker color, mix colors, or marbleize if desired.

5. Wrap bead around a plastic straw piece. Shape it into one of the following forms: sphere, cone, cylinder, cube, rectangular prism, pyramid, or elongated sphere.

6. Make quantities of each bead form according to the plan. Air-dry beads at least 24 hours.

Process: Session 3 20-30 min.

Design the necklace

7. Sort similar beads into piles. String beads on cotton cord according to the bead design plan. Check the accuracy of the pattern.

8. Tape the cord ends together for wearing.

| **Assessment** | • Ask students to identify the patterns in their classmates' necklaces. Each child creates a chart of patterns observed on five or more classmates' necklaces. Write student names in one column. Draw or write about the pattern that is repeated in each necklace. | • Students create multiplication flashcards to correspond with their necklaces. Play matching games to identify bead patterns and the multiplication facts they represent. Check for accuracy. | • Students exchange necklaces and write algebraic expressions for bead patterns. • Chart patterns, including a column to record what each variable represents (specific shape, color, or size of bead written as a =, b =, c =). Check for accuracy. |

• Ask students to reflect on this lesson and write a DREAM statement to summarize the most important things they learned.

| **Extensions** | Provide opportunities for children to make and read different kinds of patterns. Clap patterns for children to echo during transition times. Gather items for children to sort and arrange into patterns, such as crayons, recycled plastic containers, and natural objects such as shells. Some children with special needs might represent their bead patterns with small table blocks or plastic beads first. See Merry Math Patterns on Crayola.com for a whole-class patterning activity. Suggest children interview family members who may remember love beads. What stories can they share about the beads? | Children work in teams to create multiple bead strands. Begin by sketching a visual of multiples patterns. See Skip Counting on Crayola.com. Use the number grid and white Model Magic compound to create 100 small beads. Create a color code for multiples of 2, 3, 4, 5, 6, 7, 8, 9, and 10 (one color for each). Write numbers on beads. Add dots or stripes of color to demonstrate multiples. Some beads will have one color. Others may have several (numeral 24). Prime numbers will have no color at all. | Host a bead market. Assign monetary values to different bead shapes or colors. Use algebraic equations to determine the price of each student love bead necklace. Repeat activity with different prices. Suggest that gifted students explore bead-making traditions from around the world. Use algebra skills to represent different beading styles. Check out African Trade Beads on Crayola.Com to find out how to make rolled-paper beads. |

A Bountiful Table—Fair-Share Fractions

Objectives

Students create concrete, realistic, geometric drawings of food to use to explore the concept of equal or fair shares.

Students use fractions to divide their art into sets to demonstrate their understanding of fractions at a complexity appropriate to their grade level.

Multiple Intelligences

Interpersonal	Logical-mathematical
Intrapersonal	Spatial

National Standards

Visual Arts Standard #5	Mathematics Standards
Reflects upon and assesses the characteristics and merits of their work and the work of others	**Number and Operations** Understand numbers, ways of representing numbers, relationships among numbers, and number systems **Geometry** Use visualization, spatial reasoning, and geometric modeling to solve problems **Problem Solving** Apply and adapt a variety of appropriate strategies to solve problems **Representation** Create and use representations to organize, record, and communicate mathematical ideas

Background Information

Everyday objects were often the subjects of Wayne Thiebaud's still-life paintings. His painterly depictions of cakes and pies are especially well known. Unlike much 1960s Pop Art that satirically depicted consumerism in the United States, Thiebaud's paintings seem to be nostalgic and reverent. Thiebaud exploited the physical properties of paint. He captured the look and feel of the substance depicted, such as icing on cakes, by applying thick layers. Thiebaud described this palpable, sensuous employment of paint as "object transference."

Resources

Behind the Scenes Series: Vol. V, Wayne Thiebaud: Line.
Hosted by Penn and Teller
Delightful look at line with the help of illusionists Penn and Teller. All ages enjoy watching the artist Wayne Thiebaud create a drawing of an ice cream cone using line. (DVD/VHS, distributed by GPN, 28:29 min.)

Counting With Wayne Thiebaud by Susan Rubin
Presents the concepts of counting and number with Thiebaud's drawings, etchings, and paintings of multiple sweet treats. A perfect introduction to any early elementary lesson on art, fractions, and sharing.

The National Gallery of Art: www.nga.gov (search the site for "Thiebaud")

Wayne Thiebaud: A Paintings Retrospective by Steven A. Nash with Adam Gopnik
Brings together 120 of Thiebaud's paintings, pastels, and watercolors. Full-color illustrations capture students of all ages. Older students and adults will also learn much about Thiebaud's impact on art history.

Vocabulary List

Use this list to explore new vocabulary, create idea webs, or brainstorm related subjects.

Fairness
Fractions
  Eighths
  Fifths
Half
  Musical notes
  Time
  U.S. currency
Proportion
Quarter
  Liquid measures
  Musical notes
  U.S. currency

Sevenths
Shape
Sharing
Sixths
Texture
Thirds
Foot
Yard

Artwork by students from
Wood Creek Elementary School,
Farmington Hills, Michigan.
Teacher: Lynn Schatzel

A Bountiful Table—Fair-Share Fractions

	K-2	3-4	5-6
Suggested Preparation and Discussion	Ask students what *sharing* means to them. Discuss how an apple or a pizza could be shared. Offer example situations, such as eight people and one apple. Invite students to explain how they could divide the apple so every person gets a fair share. Use paper circles to demonstrate equivalent fractions. Brainstorm other foods or sets of items that could be divided fairly into parts (watermelon, loaf of bread, oranges). How would you divide each fairly for two people, three, seven, or for the whole class? For younger students and those with some types of learning disabilities, place a clear transparency over a large image of a food that could be divided, such as a loaf of bread. Invite students to use a Gel Marker as if it were a knife to "cut" the food into slices, fairly divided for a given number of people. Wipe off and repeat to "cut" a variety of different fractions. For older and more advanced students, reverse the process and estimate how many whole foods are needed to divide to feed a large group of people. Chefs plan in advance how much food to prepare. Display prints of cake paintings by Wayne Thiebaud. Describe the shape of these desserts, pizzas, and other favorite foods when looking down on them from above (circle, rectangle, square, oval).		
	Divide into groups of three or four. Each student thinks of a dessert or a healthier food. Explain that foods will be divided so that everyone in the group gets a fair share of every one.	Divide into groups of four to seven. (Odd numbers are more challenging.) Explain that each team will create oil pastel art to illustrate a table filled with foods. Teams divide their foods into equivalent fractional quantities so that there are enough pieces to serve to everyone in their group.	Divide into large groups with eight or more. Each group will create a buffet of "foods" to share. Challenge teams to create enough food so there are enough slices to serve everyone multiple pieces. How many whole items are needed to feed the large group?
Crayola® Supplies	• Erasable Crayons • Markers • Oil Pastels • Scissors		
Other Materials	• Drawing paper • Paper plates • Paper towels		
Set-up/Tips	• Erasable Crayons are recommended to create simple shapes that can be erased and redrawn as needed. Pencil sketches often lead to drawings with small details that are a challenge to fill in with oil pastels. • Demonstrate how to use a bit of paper towel or cotton swab to blend oil pastel colors. • Show students how to gently brush pastel crumbs into the trash.		

Pizza pie that is cut into segments shows parts of a whole.

Cakes cut into segments showing fraction cuts.

	K-2	3-4	5-6

Process: Session 1 20-30 min.

Draw and divide foods into equivalent parts

1. Suggest that students imagine they are looking down at the top of a table filled with foods. Fill drawing paper with erasable crayon outlines of food as if seen from above.

2. Draw lines to divide foods so each person in the group can receive a fair share.

3. Exchange drawings with classmates to check for dividing accuracy. Erase and redraw lines as needed to make all shares equal.

Process: Session 2 20-30 min.

Use oil pastels to decorate

4. Fill line drawings with oil pastel colors. Encourage children to use color-blending techniques to achieve realistic effects.

5. Decorate foods with designs, such as those found on fancy desserts or fun arrangements of pizza toppings.

Process: Session 3 20-30 min.

Slice and "serve" equivalent fractional parts

6. Cut foods into fair-share fractions according to the number of children in the group. Place each piece on a paper plate. Arrange plates of divided foods on a table or desks.

7. Groups divide each other's foods among their plates so everyone has an equal share. Talk about how it feels to have fair shares. Return foods to the original plates.

8. Divide food among plates so the shares are unfair. Ask students to talk about how they feel about unfair shares. Have students switch plates with each other to see other points of view. How could the amount of food available be divided so that each person does get a fair share?

9. Identify the fractional parts with their correct names and symbols by writing on the back of each piece.

Assessment

- Assess division of each student's food into accurate, fair fractions.

- Observe the process of determining fair and unfair shares in each group. Do students use mathematical reasoning to divide the foods fairly? How convincingly do they present their viewpoints?

- Children write or orally describe their foods and the way they were divided into equivalent fractional quantities using accurate names and symbols.

- Ask students to reflect on this lesson and write a DREAM statement to summarize the most important things they learned.

Extensions

Younger children and students with special needs might begin by dividing actual foods so they have a relevant concrete experience before working with representations.

Hold an international foods buffet in which families share their favorite ethnic dishes with small groups of children. Children determine when the foods are appropriately divided among participants.

Incorporate a gourmet chef contest into the lesson. Students create ballots and vote on criteria for their foods such as these.

- Drawing that has the most elaborately decorated foods.

- Drawing that has the most unique way to divide the desserts equally.

Find out about careers as food stylists, chefs, and restaurant managers, for example. What mathematical skills are necessary for these positions?

In what other ways are foods represented in the arts? Consider still-life paintings from various time periods and parts of the world. What do those depictions reveal about the culture, setting, and artist?

Challenge gifted students to create fraction games using the pieces they created. Game objectives could be to identify, compare, add, subtract, multiply, or divide fractions.

Division diagrams show 1/2, 1/4, 1/8 and 1/16 of a whole circle.

Division diagrams show 1/3, 1/5 and 1/7 of a whole circle.

Crayola Dream~Makers®
Building fun and creativity into standards-based learning

Objectives

Students explain increasingly complex relationships between visual arts, mathematics, and the cultures, times, and locations of Native American peoples.

Students create replicas of Native American handiwork that they use to chart, estimate, check, and analyze colored bead data.

Multiple Intelligences

Interpersonal
Logical-mathematical
Spatial

What Does It Mean?

Curiosities: rare or novel objects or ideas

Whimsy: fanciful beaded ornament created by Native American artists for souvenirs

National Standards

Visual Arts Standard #4	**Mathematics Standards**
Understands the visual arts in relation to history and culture	***Number and Operations*** Compute fluently and make reasonable estimates ***Problem Solving*** Apply and adapt a variety of appropriate strategies to solve problems ***Representation*** Create and use representations to organize, record, and communicate mathematical ideas

Background Information

Native American women in many nations were skilled in beadwork. To economically survive in a changing world, enterprising women of the Iroquois nation, particularly from the Mohawk and Tuscarora tribes, designed and crafted beaded items to sell to tourists in the late 1800s through early 1900s. These items, particularly pincushions, became quite popular as souvenirs at places such as Niagara Falls.

"Beaded whimsies," as they are now often called, were made in shapes such as hearts, canoes, and fancy, high-top shoes. Their stuffed fabric bases were embellished with seed and bugle beads in a wide array of hues. Motifs included birds, flowers, leaves, and the U.S. flag. Sometimes they were emblazoned with dates and the names of travel destinations. Very few of the designs were typical of the motifs used on the Native Americans' own beaded items. Instead they were shrewdly designed to specifically appeal to the gaudy tastes of Victorian tourists.

Resources

Beaded Critters by Sonal Bhatt
Inspiring how-to book for ages 9 and up. Photographs of colorful bead animal embellishments reminiscent of those found on "beaded whimsies."

Trading Identities by Ruth B. Phillips
Images and historical anecdotes introduce older students to art forms produced by Native Americans for tourists in northeastern United States.

Vocabulary List

Use this list to explore new vocabulary, create idea webs, or brainstorm related subjects.

- Data-recording techniques
  Charts & graphs
    Bar
    Circle
    Flow chart
    Picture
  Checklists
  Counting

  Music
    Notes
    Staff
    Tally marks

- Native American art
  Famous contemporary artists
    Alan Houser
    Clementine Hunter
    Edmonia Lewis
    Jaune Quick-to-See Smith
  Traditional techniques
    Beadwork
    Pottery
  Tourist trade
    Baskets
    Curiosities
    Toys
    Whimsy

"1905" Hanging
Picture Frame
Beaded Whimsy
Circa early 1900s
High-relief glass beading on shocking pink cotton field
10" x 6 1/4"
Collection of Dr. Thomas Schantz.

"From Niagara Falls" Hanging Shoe
Pincushion Whimsy
Circa early 1900s
Glass beading on purple velvet field
7 1/2" x 6 1/4" x 2 1/4"
Collection of Dr. Thomas Schantz.

Artwork by students from
Sandy Plains Elementary School,
Baltimore, Maryland.
Teachers: Jen O'Flaherty, Rob Bartoch

104
63

25
24

20
31

Artwork created by students from
St. Theresa School,
Hellertown, Pennsylvania.

Crayola

Dream~Makers®
Building fun and creativity into standards-based learning

Whimsical Charting and Checking

	K-2	3-4	5-6
Suggested Preparation and Discussion	Share information and pictures of Native American beadwork. Some created beaded pincushion whimsies to sell to tourists. Ask students to discuss how these crafters may have tracked the number of beads needed to plan for each design. Craft a sample relevant whimsy to inspire student creativity.		
	Show children the sample whimsy. Ask how they might record the number of beads of each color so they could make more identical whimsies. Together, chart the number of beads of each color using tally marks or picture symbols.	Ask students to suggest ways to tally numerical data. If they were bead artists, how might they record the number of beads it takes to cover a small bag? Explain how to create a chart to record estimates as well as actual number of beads used. Create personal charts to estimate and tally colors of beads used in their own artwork. Ask how they might calculate the total number of beads used by the entire class, including how many of each color were used.	
	Each child makes a blank chart similar to the one created together. Shade in or write names of colors as headings. Include spaces to estimate, tally, and record the number of beads of each color and the total beads used.	Create a class chart with one row for each student and columns labeled with colors to chart, estimate, and total beading whimsies.	Students work together to determine and record the total number of beads the class used in their combined projects as well as how many of each color they used. Brainstorm, define tasks, form teams, and create materials needed to organize and record data.
Crayola® Supplies	• Colored Pencils • Glitter Glue (optional) • Markers • Model Magic® • School Glue • Scissors		
Other Materials	• Modeling tools • Ribbon, yarn, or string • Ruler • White paper		
Set-up/Tips	• Add color to white Model Magic compound using washable markers. • Use scissors to cut flattened Model Magic shapes. • Glue beads to the form. Glue ribbon to Model Magic whimsy.		

"Fox Box" With Lid and Handles Beaded Whimsy
Circa early 1900s
Glass beading on electric pink cotton field
7" x 5 1/2" x 8" including loops
Collection of Dr. Thomas Schantz.

Tri-lobe Heart Hanging Pincushion Whimsy
Circa early 1900s
Glass beading on pink field
8" x 8 1/4" x 3"
Collection of Dr. Thomas Schantz.

	K-2	3-4	5-6
Process: Session 1 20-30 min.	**Design cushion** 1. Draw a simple geometric shape (circle, triangle, square) on a 3- x 4-inch paper.	**Design cushion** 1. Outline a shape (heart, star, shell) on a 3- x 4-inch paper.	**Design cushion** 1. Outline an interesting shape (flower, bird, turtle) on 3- x 4-inch paper.
	2. Draw at least one more shape inside the original. 3. Show students how to create a beading pattern by filling the cushion with colored dots. Draw dots to form patterns.		
Process: Session 2 40-60 min.	**Make the whimsy** 4. Form a tennis-ball amount of Model Magic compound into the cushion. 5. Cut 10-inch ribbons. Knot ends. Poke one end of the loop into the top of the cushion. Glue in place. 6. Roll tiny Model Magic beads. Glue colored spheres to the cushion. Apply glitter glue for dramatic effects if desired. Air-dry whimsies 24 hours.		
Process: Session 3 20-30 min.	**Estimate, chart, and check** 7. Children estimate the total number of beads on their whimsies as well as the number of each color. Record on individual charts. 8. Children count and record the number of beads of each color on their whimsies. 9. Children count each other's beads to check accuracy. What similarities and differences did they notice?	**Estimate, chart, and check** 7. Students estimate the total number of beads and the number of beads of each color in their designs. Record on individual charts.	
		8. Add individual estimates to class chart. Total estimates for all beads and each color.	8. Follow the plan for gathering class estimation data.
		9. Count the number of each color of beads used. Record on individual and class charts.	9. Gather class bead-usage data according to student plan.
		10. Students check each other's data for accuracy. Analyze and discuss findings.	
Assessment			• How effectively did students in grades 5 and 6 contribute to creation of a class plan for tallying results?
	• Compare individual and group data charts with actual bead designs. • Ask students to reflect on this lesson and write a DREAM statement to summarize the most important things they learned.		
Extensions	Use finished whimsies to provide additional practice in estimating, counting, and recording data. Work in pairs to estimate, check, and record data for several whimsies. Younger students and those with some types of learning disabilities could use beads to work on sorting and classification skills.	Students create plans for half-size whimsy replicas. Use previous data to estimate the number of beads needed for these versions. Write directions, trade directions with classmates, and follow them to create replicas. Count and record actual number of beads used. Compare actual numbers with estimates.	Look for patterns in the data. Challenge students to compare different designs and data patterns to form hypotheses about the data. Are there factors that lead one whimsy to have a higher count of beads than another? Identify those factors and test hypotheses.
	Encourage a simple, large design and the use of large beads rather than tiny ones for students whose fine-motor skills are not yet fully developed. Challenge advanced students with an interest in research to find out more about other forms of Native American beadwork and report their findings to the class.		

Shaping Up With Shapes

Objectives

Students identify, compare, and contrast shapes, and shapes within shapes, in artistic compositions.

Students make and use shape stamps to create Paul Klee-like compositions featuring overlapping images.

Students in grades K to 2 use spatial reasoning skills to count the number of times each shape appears in their artistic compositions.

Students in grades 3 and 4 use measuring tools to determine and chart the perimeters of shapes within their artistic compositions.

Students in grades 5 and 6 use measuring tools and spatial reasoning skills to determine the total area covered by similar shapes within their artistic compositions.

Multiple Intelligences

Logical-mathematical

Spatial

What Does It Mean?

Color gradation: passing of one tint or shade of color to another by very small (barely perceptible) degrees

Color value: relative lightness or darkness of a color

National Standards

Visual Arts Standard #1	Mathematics Standards
Understands and applies media, techniques, and processes	**Geometry** Use visualization, spatial reasoning, and geometric modeling to solve problems **Reasoning** Recognize reasoning and proof as fundamental aspects of mathematics *Grades 3-6* **Measurement** Apply appropriate techniques, tools, and formulas to determine measurements

Background Information

During the 1920s, Swiss artist Paul Klee often spattered watercolor over stencils and netting. When Klee taught at the Bauhaus (a famous German art school), he experimented with this technique. The effect is shown in *Glance of a Landscape*. In this work, Klee applied brushstrokes of pale gray opaque watercolor on top of transparent watercolor that was spattered broadly to create trees. Klee usually mounted his drawings on cardboard, which was where he wrote the title and date for this composition.

Resources

Dreaming Pictures: Paul Klee by Paul Klee
Klee's dream world is made accessible through this tour of his compelling artwork. Children's comments and questions add to the enjoyment.

Echoes for the Eye: Poems to Celebrate Patterns in Nature by Barbara Esbensen
Compilation of poems and lovely watercolor illustrations. Draws attention to the repetition of shapes and patterns in the natural world.

Shape Patterns by Marion Smoothey
Investigates the world of shapes, then offers fun activities for drawing, measuring, and using them.

Vocabulary List

Use this list to explore new vocabulary, create idea webs, or brainstorm related subjects.

Area	Line	Rhythms
Balance	Linear figures	Rotation
Color	Motion	Shape
Color fields	Movement	Texture
Composition	Patten	Transformations
Emphasis	Perimeter	Unity
Enlargements	Proportion	Value
Form	Reflections	Variety
Gradations	Repetition	

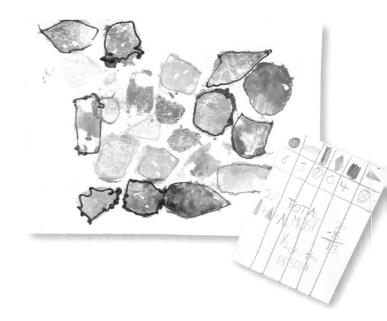

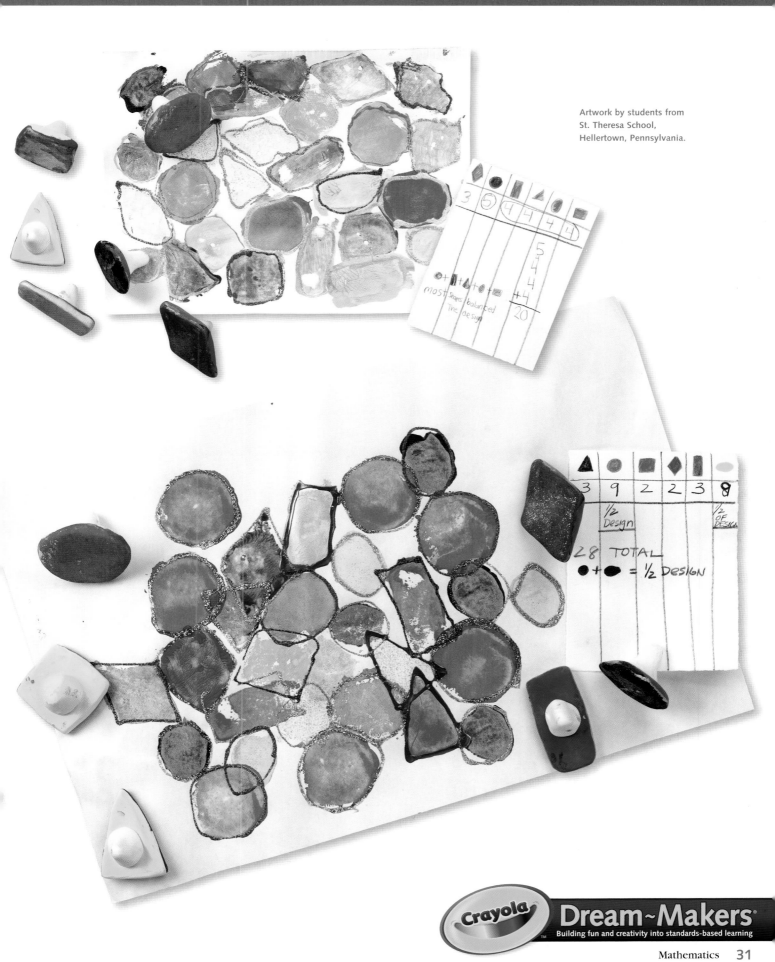

Artwork by students from
St. Theresa School,
Hellertown, Pennsylvania.

Shaping Up With Shapes

	K-2	3-4	5-6
Suggested Preparation and Discussion	Create a wall poster depicting a square grid: 4 rows of 4 squares each. Invite children to search for and count all of the squares they see in the poster.		
	Ask a student volunteer to outline each of the 16 small squares in the grid, writing a numeral inside each square. Challenge children to find other squares. Help children see the largest square (the entire grid) and squares made of 4 and 9 smaller squares. Outline those squares in another color.	Challenge students to find more than 16 squares. Ask students to explain how they can find more than 16 squares in the grid. Ask students why they think most people would see only 16 squares. Look for rectangles in much the same way. Challenge more advanced students with more complicated grids.	
	Display examples of art by Paul Klee and the sample design. Ask students to look at this artwork carefully to find shapes and patterns that others may not see. Look closely at colors to find gradations and compare color value. Discuss how looking carefully sharpens thinking and can assist in solving problems. Create sample shape stamps and a large sample design with overlapping shapes.		
Crayola® Supplies	• Glitter Glue • Model Magic® • Paint Brushes • Scissors • Tempera Paint		
Other Materials	• Drawing paper • Hand-held pencil sharpeners • Modeling tools (such as craft sticks, markers, and plastic knives) • Paper towels • Recycled newspaper • Water containers		
		• Rulers	
Set-up/Tips	• Cover painting surface with recycled newspaper.		
Process: Session 1 5-10 min.	**Create stamps** 1. Flatten Model Magic compound with hands or roll with a marker barrel. Make it thick enough to pick up easily. 2. Children cut shapes (triangle, parallelogram, rhombus) appropriate to their geometric skills. Air-dry 24 hours.		

Farmers Market Produce
Photo by R. De Long

Chihuly Glass Shapes
Photo by R. De Long

	K-2	3-4	5-6
Process: Session 2 40-60 min.	**Stamp shapes** 3. Brush paint colors on flat side of a shape. Press stamp, paint side down, on paper. Lift stamp. Repeat using different paint colors. Flip or turn the shape so it appears in a variety of places and angles in the design. Observe color effects. 4. Exchange shapes with classmates. Repeat stamping. Overlap several different shapes and colors. Air-dry the paint.		
Process: Session 3 10-15 min.	**Outline shapes** 5. Outline several shapes with glitter glue to enrich the surface design. Air-dry the glue.		
Process: Session 4 20-30 min.	**Count shapes** 6. Use the sample design to demonstrate how to count shapes. Remind students that shapes may have been flipped or turned, but they still remain the same shape. 7. Show children how to create a simple chart to record the number of each shape in their artwork. 8. Count and record the number of each shape on their own artwork.	**Count and chart shapes** 6. Ask students to identify all of the shapes in their artwork. 7. Create charts to show the number of each shape in the compositions. 8. Use measuring tools to determine the perimeter of each shape in the design. Add information to chart. 9. Total the length of all perimeters.	8. Challenge students to determine the area covered by each shape in their design. Add information to chart. 9. Calculate the area covered by the overlapping shapes.
Assessment	• Exchange finished designs with a partner. Partners add up the total number of shapes they see in the finished art. Check to see if their counts match.	• Compare designs with a partner. How are they similar and how are they different? Compare the types and sizes of shapes that appear in each design. Compare similar shapes to see which is larger and smaller. Compare colors in similar shapes. Estimate sizes, then measure to check. Record comparison results on paper to display with both designs.	• Students create charts with spaces for recording total area covered by each shape in their designs as a "quiz" for a partner. Exchange finished designs. Partners measure and calculate the area covered by each shape in the design. Compare results with the design's creator.
	• Ask students to reflect on this lesson and write a DREAM statement to summarize the most important things they learned.		
Extensions	Repeat this technique using other shapes such as leaves, letters, or paper cut-out handprints. Flip, slide, and turn stamps for different effects. Make shape pattern puzzles on long strips of paper. Use the stamps to make repeating patterns for a partner to analyze and finish. (Example: square, square, triangle, square...)	Brainstorm real-life reasons to measure perimeter. Borrow a book of children's wallpaper borders. Each student chooses a favorite. Challenge the class to measure the perimeters of the gym or cafeteria. How many feet of border are needed to decorate the walls all the way around? How many rolls are needed? Challenge students to measure the perimeters of other shapes, including doorways, rugs, or furniture. See Metric Hugs on Crayola.com.	Combine stamps into a corporate work of art. Students work together to brainstorm, choose, and plan large shapes to cut from posterboard and cover with stamps. Challenge students to do calculations in advance. Encourage gifted students to measure and calculate areas of increasingly irregular shapes.
	To enable students with special needs to more readily see shapes within shapes, encourage them to outline each shape with a different color so the overlapping images can be seen more easily. Challenge students to find congruent parts within each other's compositions.		

Toying Around With Geometry

Objectives

Students create functional, wheeled 3-D toys reflecting spatial reasoning skills with geometric forms.

Students draw and label the pictures (K-2, 5-6) or write and illustrate toy package inserts (3-4) describing geometric attributes of their structures to demonstrate their understanding of the way parts were used in the invention process.

Multiple Intelligences

Linguistic
Logical-mathematical
Spatial

What Does It Mean?

Corner: where three or more edges meet

Edge: location where two plane figures meet

Plane figures: flat, 2-D images of geometric shapes

Space figures: 3-D geometric forms such as spheres, cubes, and cones

National Standards

Visual Arts Standard #2	Mathematics Standards
Using knowledge of structures and functions	**Connections** Understand how mathematical ideas interconnect and build on one another to produce a coherent whole **Geometry** Analyze characteristics and properties of two- and three-dimensional geometric shapes and develop mathematical arguments about geometric relationship **Communication** Communicate their mathematical thinking coherently and clearly to peers, teachers, and others **Measurement** Apply appropriate techniques, tools, and formulas to determine measurements **Problem Solving** Solve problems that arise in mathematics and in other contexts **Representation** Use representations to model and interpret physical, social, and mathematical phenomena

Background Information

Toys are an important part of children's lives because they stimulate young minds. Toys help children learn important concepts, develop motor and thinking skills, and express their personalities. In many cultures, play is also viewed as a preparation for life. With Native American children, for example, each traditional toy carries a unique legacy of history, tradition, design, and practical technique. Perhaps one of the first toys, dating back to 6000 BCE, was a game of chess, which evolved from an Indian game called Chaturanga.

In Europe during the 1300s to 1500s, many toys were destroyed in an effort to eliminate the spread of the Bubonic plague. Combined with the wear and tear of time, it is difficult to find antique toys from periods before the 16th century.

Alexander Calder was fascinated by motion and created handcrafted toys early in his art career. He and other artists designed forms and shapes with moveable parts. Their art, including famous mobiles, considered fun by many, moves and delights the eyes and minds of children of all ages.

Resources

Dolls and Toys of Native America—A Journey Through Childhood by Don & Debra McQuiston
Beautiful full-color images with text describe how toys taught Native American children their life skills while bringing them delight and joy.

Roarr: Calder's Circus by Maira Kalman
An introduction to Alexander Calder and his tiny, playful circus. Inspires children of all ages to be creative and have fun while using their problem-solving skills.

Vocabulary List

Use this list to explore new vocabulary, create idea webs, or brainstorm related subjects.

- Art terms

  Armature
  Form
  Glaze
  Joining

  Original
  Shape
  Texture

- Favorite toys

  Analyze
    3-D forms
      Corners
      Edges
      Planes
  Construction methods
  Mobile/stationary

  Compare/contrast
    Hand-made toys
    Manufactured items

- Package insert

  Name of toy
    Geometric terms
    Alliteration
    Onomatopoeia

  Diagram
  Draw
  Label

- Simple machines

  Inclined planes
  Levers
  Wheels/axles

- Space figures

  Cone
  Cube
  Cylinder
  Pyramid
  Rectangular prism
  Sphere

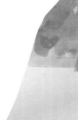

Steam Powered Shovel Toy
Circa 1931
Fabricated tin and cotton cord
20" x 7" x 14"
Collection of Rudy Clark.

"Andy Gump" Toy
Circa 1930s
Cast iron
7 1/4" x 3 3/4" x 6"
Collection
of Rudy Clark.

Artwork by students from
John J. Jennings Elementary School,
Bristol, Connecticut.
Teacher: Barbara Grasso

Crayola **Dream~Makers**
Building fun and creativity into standards-based learning

Toying Around With Geometry

	K-2	3-4	5-6
Suggested Preparation and Discussion	Display 3-D figures (or images of them) including a sphere, pyramid, rectangular prism, cube, cone, and cylinder. Ask students to describe what they see. Lead children to discover that all 3-D (or *space* figures) combine flat 2-D (or *plane* figures). A cube consists of six flat squares. The locations where two plane figures meet are called *edges*. Areas where three or more edges meet are called *corners*. Look for plane figures, edges, and corners in the displayed objects and other common items. Focus on using geometric vocabulary.		
	Look at several samples of toy packages. Does what is displayed on the outside of the package always match what is inside? Share experiences with toys that need to be assembled.		
	Analyze a moveable toy with axles, wheels, and a simple body. Ask children to figure out how the toy works and how the parts of the toy function to make it move. Count the wheels. Point out the axle(s) on which the wheels rotate. Ask children to identify the plane and space figures that make the toy's body. If possible, take the toy apart to demonstrate how the parts make up the whole toy.		
	Challenge students to design an original, wheeled, moveable toy (for display only) that can be built with plane and space figures such as recycled materials and Model Magic®. Children decide how many wheels, axles, and other moving parts their inventions will have. This toy will be part of a "kit" for which they will also prepare a "package insert."		
	Ask children to identify what space figure/form a drinking straw represents (cylinder). What 2-D shape can be seen when looking at the end of a straw? (circle) Repeat with other forms as needed to expand their geometry vocabulary.		

Crayola® Supplies	• Gel Markers • Model Magic® • Paint Brushes • School Glue • Scissors

Other Materials	• Chenille stems • Decorative craft items (such as toothpicks, buttons, feathers) • Dowel sticks (1/8-inch diameter) • Large paper clips • Modeling tools such as plastic dinner knives, craft sticks, and toothpicks • Plastic drinking straws • Recycled plastic beverage bottles or other clean, found objects • Recycled foam produce trays • Rulers • String, ribbon, or yarn • Water containers • White paper

Set-up/Tips	• Ask students and their families to collect clean recycled items. • By its nature, wood is rough and may contain splinters. Ask parent volunteers to cut dowel sticks into varying lengths. • Remind children that the toys they create are for display only—they are not recommended for use. • Encourage students to use their imaginations. Offer strategies, modeling techniques, and ideas to support student innovations. • Model Magic fresh from the pack sticks to itself. Use glue to strengthen Model Magic seams and joints. • Show children how to construct moveable axles by inserting a dowel stick into a straw. Push wheels on the ends of the dowels.

Process: Session 1 20-30 min.	### Create axles and wheels 1. Measure and cut straws into the desired lengths for axles. 2. Choose dowel rods that are about 3 inches longer than the straws. Insert the dowels into the straws. 3. Roll and flatten Model Magic® compound into wheels. 4. Push wheels on the ends of dowels. Air-dry the wheels.

Process: Session 2 20-30 min.	### Build the body of the toy 5. Choose an armature upon which to build the toy, such as a plastic bottle or cardboard box. 6. Build up the body by attaching plane figures cut from recycled items to the armature with Model Magic slabs. Overlap edges and glue sections to the bottle as needed for reinforcement. Add texture and decorative elements with Model Magic bits and modeling tools. 7. Attach axles to the body. One way to do this is to press strips of Model Magic over the straws onto the underside of the armature. 8. Tie string to one end of a paper clip. Glue the other end of the paper clip and embed it in Model Magic compound on the front of the toy. Air-dry the construction for 24 hours.

	K-2	3-4	5-6
Process: Session 3 20-30 min.	**Add details** 9. Embellish the toy with ribbon, toothpicks, chenille stems, and other craft items. Attach with glue. Air-dry the glue. 10. Decorate the toy using gel markers. 11. Mix a glaze of equal parts glue and water. Brush the glaze over the Model Magic. Air-dry the toy.		
Process: Session 4 30-40 min.	**Draw and label picture** 12. Look carefully at the toy. Draw all of the 3-D forms and 2-D planes used to construct the toy. 13. Draw a picture of the finished toy. Label the 2-D planes and 3-D forms. One method is to draw an arrow to one part of the toy and then draw the plane shape to which the arrow points. Older children also write geometric terms for the shapes and forms.	**Write package inserts** 12. List all of the 3-D forms and planes used to construct the toy. 13. Diagram and label all plane and space figures used to create the toy. 14. Write step-by-step directions explaining how to construct the toy as if it were a kit to be assembled.	**Draw detailed diagrams** 12. Draw the toy and label the diagram (including specific space and plane figures, edges, and corners) in detail from at least three different angles, such as looking at figure from above, from below, head on, from the back, left side, right side, or underneath.
Assessment	• Are the toys wheeled and movable? • Ask students to reflect on this lesson and write a DREAM statement to summarize the most important things they learned.		
	• How original are the toys? Did children creatively use the armatures, modeling materials, and embellishments to invent their toys? • Observe children's abilities to communicate both verbally and on paper about the construction of their toys. • Can children correctly name basic 2-D shapes and 3-D forms?	• Review both toy and package insert, informally interviewing children to assess their awareness of space figures, plane figures, and spatial reasoning. • Is the package insert drawn with detail? Are toy parts labeled correctly? • Are the assembly directions clear and in chronological order?	• Interview students about their toys, referring to drawings and labels, to determine their ability to identify plane and space figures and their positions in space. • Are the three perspective drawings accurate and detailed?
Extensions	Younger children and those with special needs might enjoy creating these toys with the assistance of family members, either in the classroom or at home. Take toys "on the road" for a toy parade. Invite school staff, parents, and other friends and relatives to the classroom. Or visit other classrooms to show student creations. Pair each toy inventor with a visitor so the inventor can tell how he or she made the toy. Ask visitors to share positive feedback about the toys with the inventors. Keep the toy factory rolling! See Crayola.com to make Hollyhock Dolls and Quack, Moo, and Oink Finger Puppets, for example. Provide materials for children to independently invent their own robots from recycled cereal boxes. Check out the Accordion-Arm Robot on Crayola.com for inspiration.	Invite children to think of names for their toys based on the toy's geometric design. Work in teams to create ad campaigns for the toys. Write jingles, design print ads, and/or produce radio and television ads. Set up a toy fair in the classroom to display toys, inserts, and advertisements. Invite children from neighboring classrooms to visit the toy fair. Survey them as they leave about which three toys they would most like to buy. Tally and talk about the results. Find out about the creative inventions of Leonardo DaVinci. Let his creative ideas inspire more designs. See the Recycle Inventions Lesson Plan on Crayola.com for ideas.	How do the toys measure up? Challenge gifted students to measure each toy's height, weight, length, width, rolling speed from point to point, and other characteristics. Create comparison lists, ranking toys by various measures (tallest, widest, heaviest, fastest). Research inventions and inventors. Find out how some inventions came about accidentally while others have a history of effort behind them. Compile research into visual and written reports for an Invention Hall of Fame. See Crayola.com for an Activity Page to start the research.

Measure Twice, Create Once

Objectives

Students apply skill-level appropriate techniques and tools to determine the real size of objects using standard and nonstandard units of measure.

Students apply mathematics and problem-solving skills to create scale drawings of objects.

Multiple Intelligences

Bodily-kinesthetic
Interpersonal
Logical-mathematical
Spatial

What Does It Mean?

Cubit: principal unit of measurement in ancient Egypt, equal to 52.4 cm

Petroglyph: drawing or carving on rock created by prehistoric people

Pictograph: artwork that shows people, places, and/or things in pictures, signs, or symbols

National Standards

Visual Arts Standard #1
Understands and applies media, techniques, and processes

Mathematics Standards
Measurement
Understand measurable attributes of objects and the units, systems, and processes of measurement
Connections
Recognize and apply mathematics in contexts outside of mathematics

Background Information

The Ancient Egyptians incorporated a measurement system into all fundamental areas of their lives, including commerce, building, and art.

Using body parts with which to measure, the Egyptian measurement system included units such as the *cubit* (the length of a man's arm from elbow to tip of middle finger), *palm* (cross-wise width of hand), and *span* (the length of outstretched upper limbs).

Graphic artists use the human head as the basic unit of measurement for drawing the entire body in proportion. The height of the head from the chin to the top of the head is the "ruler" by which vertical lines in a human form are measured. Fine artists often consider that most people are 7.5 head lengths tall.

One way archaeologists record prehistoric petroglyphs and pictographs is to carefully create a string grid over the petroglyphs or artifacts and then do a scaled-down sketch on paper of what they see in each square.

Resources

Math Curse by Jon Scieszka & Lane Smith
Humorous look at numbers in everyday life, including measurement, time, arithmetic, and problem-solving. All ages.

Picasso's One-Liners by Pablo Picasso
A collection of Picasso's one-liners, drawings created in one movement, without lifting drawing tool from paper. All ages.

The Painter by Peter Catalanotto
A celebration of creativity in life and art. Cover illustration shows a father tracing his child's body on large paper. Simple text and vivid watercolor illustrations appeal to young children.

Concept List

Use this list to explore new vocabulary, create idea webs, or brainstorm related subjects.

- Nonstandard units of measure
  Paper clips   Index cards

- Terms
  Height   Length   Width

- Units of measure – Length

Metric	U.S. Customary	Egyptian
Centimeter	Foot	Cubit
Kilometer	Inch	Palm
Meter	Mile	Span
Millimeter	Yard	

- Scale

Models	Drawings	Archaeology
Cars	Book illustrations	Digs
Globes	Maps	Petroglyphs
Trains	Scientific illustrations	Pictographs

Artwork by students from Spring Garden Elementary School, Bethlehem, Pennsylvania.
Teacher: Pat Check

Artwork by students from
St. Theresa School,
Hellertown, Pennsylvania.

Artwork by students from
Spring Garden Elementary School,
Bethlehem, Pennsylvania.
Teacher: Pat Check

Crayola

Dream~Makers®
Building fun and creativity into standards-based learning

Measure Twice, Create Once

	K-2	3-4	5-6
Suggested Preparation and Discussion	Introduce use of hands and fingers as units of measure. Demonstrate how to determine the length of a marker by counting fingertips set side by side along the barrel. Show how to measure the length of a desk by counting palms set side by side. Invite children to measure other objects and compare results. What do they notice? Why might two different children using the same body part to measure the same object obtain different results?	Who has measured objects using ancient Egyptian units of measure? Talk about the Egyptian standards for length—the cubit, palm, and span—and how long each might be. Use a yardstick or ruler to measure body parts and shoe sizes, for example. Compare findings among students to see the variations. Talk about how that could be a challenge when building furniture or sewing clothes. Brainstorm and list different measurement units suitable for the grade level and children's skills including U.S. Customary, metric, and historic measures. Which units measure length and which measure area?	
Crayola® Supplies	• Construction Paper™ Crayons • Erasable Colored Pencils • Markers		
		• Paint Brushes • Tempera Paint	
Other Materials	• Construction paper • Rulers		
		• Craft paper on a roll • Paper plates • Paper towels • Recycled newspapers • Water containers • Yardsticks	
Set-up/Tips		• Cover painting surface with recycled newspaper. • Mix paint colors on paper plates.	
Process: Session 1 20-30 min.	**Measure and draw a grid** 1. Children measure and cut construction paper in half (4.5 x 6 inches). Lay one piece flat, vertically. Place ruler along the left edge of the paper and mark off inches starting at the top. Do the same on the right side. 2. Use a ruler to connect the marks, making rows across the paper. 3. Create 1-inch wide columns in a similar manner. 4. Number squares consecutively from left to right across the rows, starting on the top row. **Trace a hand** 5. Children place an open hand or simple shapes on a grid and trace around them with crayon, or draw a simple figure using simple shapes on the paper.	**Measure and draw a grid** 1. Children divide into small groups of three to five. Cut craft paper large enough to contain a life-size contour drawing of one student in the group. 2. Students measure and mark 3- or 4-inch square grids, depending on their skills, of columns and rows of squares on craft paper. 3. Number the squares from left to right across each row. Observe multiplication and other patterns in numbered cells at the ends of each row. **Trace a body model** 4. Each group chooses a model from the team to lie on the grid in an unusual position. 5. Team members trace around the model.	

Beside the Still Waters
1984-2003
Artist: Kendall Shaw
Acrylic and mirrors on canvas
60" x 60"
Collection of the artist.

Sun Ship
1982
Artist: Kendall Shaw
Acrylic and mirrors on canvas
4 panels, total 101" x 101"
Collection of the artist.

	K-2	3-4	5-6
Process: Session 2 30-40 min.	**Measure and draw larger, personal grids** 6. Create a grid of 2-inch squares on a full sheet of construction paper. Follow steps from Session 1, mark papers every 2 inches. Number squares in this larger grid to match the smaller grid. **Enlarge a hand** 7. Demonstrate how to copy the lines and curves that appear in the squares of the smaller grid into the corresponding squares of the larger grid.	**Measure and draw smaller, personal grids** 6. Using 12- x 18-inch construction paper, students each create an evenly spaced grid with the same number of rows, columns, and cells as on the team grid. Lightly number each cell to match the larger grid. **Reduce and redraw** 7. Show students how to draw the lines and curves that appear in the larger squares of the team grid on the corresponding smaller squares of their personal grids to create a reduced version of the figure outlined on the large craft paper.	
Process: Session 3 30-40 min.	**Add color and patterned designs to smaller grids** 8. Students fill all the shapes in their smaller grids with crayon color to enrich and personalize them.		
Process: Session 4 30-40 min.	**Paint large hand design** 9. Fill larger hand grids with colors and patterns.	**Paint team grid** 9. Fill the group grid with paint colors. Plan use of negative space to highlight the outline if desired.	
Assessment	• Assess student grids for precise measurements. • Observe the drawing process. Did students use problem-solving strategies to redraw and scale figures? • Students exchange drawings to check how well smaller drawings match larger drawings. • Ask students to reflect on this lesson and write a DREAM statement to summarize the most important things they learned.		
Extensions	Practice measuring desktops or other classroom items using a variety of units of measure such as crayons, paper clips, or yarn. Make and grid scale drawings of the desktops to represent the various units of measure. Simplify the grid-making part of this lesson for young students or those with special needs by providing cardboard "rulers" marked off in inches.	Show children sports play books created by coaches. How is scale used to create play books? How do the drawings of various plays show problem-solving strategies? Create scale drawings of favorite sports fields. The On the Court Lesson Plan found on Crayola.com offers a fun way to bring math, science, art, and sports together in a big way.	Research how archaeologists use scale plans to show the locations of discoveries and details of structures. See Pyramids in Paint on Crayola.com for an exploration of the Great Pyramids. Challenge students with strong mathematical aptitude to explore architectural blueprints (of the school if possible) and explain the scale notations and other symbols to classmates. Use problem-solving skills to determine the real sizes of the rooms and building.

To demonstrate how mural artists use grids, each child selects a photograph of a simple object or photograph depending on children's abilities. Superimpose a grid over the picture. On mural paper create a larger, proportionate grid. Create a drawing of the object using skills learned during this lesson.

It's About Time...Average Time!

Objectives

Students measure elapsed time to answer questions about average time needed to complete tasks.

Students collect, organize, analyze, and display relevant time research data.

Students in grades K-2 sketch pictures of daily tasks and record the time each task takes.

Students in grades 3-6 draw in sketchbooks and record the amount of elapsed time they draw each day.

Students design color-coded bar graphs to show the results of their research and analyze their findings.

Multiple Intelligences

- Bodily-kinesthetic
- Interpersonal
- Logical-mathematical
- Naturalist

What Does It Mean?

Mean: a mathematical average

Median: the middle point in a series of values

Mode: the value that occurs the greatest number of times in a given series

National Standards

Visual Arts Standard #3
Chooses and evaluates a range of subject matter, symbols, and ideas

Mathematics Standards
Data Analysis and Probability
Formulate questions that can be answered with data and collect, organize, and display relevant data to answer them
Measurement
Understand measurable attributes of objects and the units, systems, and processes of measurement

Background Information

Some art takes very little time to create and other art takes hours, weeks, and sometimes years. Graffiti typically takes little time and little skill to generate and many believe it creates a visual blight within cities. Some communities in the United States have found solutions that contribute visual improvements and demonstrate that artwork, even graffiti, can take time. One example of this is The Philadelphia Mural Arts Program (MAP). This public art program works in partnership with community residents, grassroots organizations, government agencies, educational institutions, corporations, and philanthropic groups to design and create murals of enduring value while actively engaging youth in the process. Those who participate in these efforts come to a clearer understanding of just how much time it takes to create art while working as a team.

Resources

All I See by Cynthia Rylant and Peter Catalanotto
A young boy's friendship with a painter inspires the way he sees the world around him. For all ages.

Counting on Frank by Rod Clement
With the help of his dog, Frank, the narrator collects math-themed facts. Appealingly illustrated, for all ages.

Vocabulary List

Use this list to explore new vocabulary, create idea webs, or brainstorm related subjects.

- Art terms

Composition	Mural
Fine art	Sketch
Graffiti	Sketchbook
Mixed media	Visual effects
Multi media	

- Calculating

Approximate	Median
Average	Mode
Estimate	Rounding
Mean	Total

- Graphing

Bar graph	Statistic
Data	Table
Pictograph	

- Telling time

Century	Duration
Day	Elapsed time
Decade	Half hour
	Half past
	Hour
	Minute
	O'clock
	Second
	Year

Artwork by students from St. Theresa School, Hellertown, Pennsylvania.

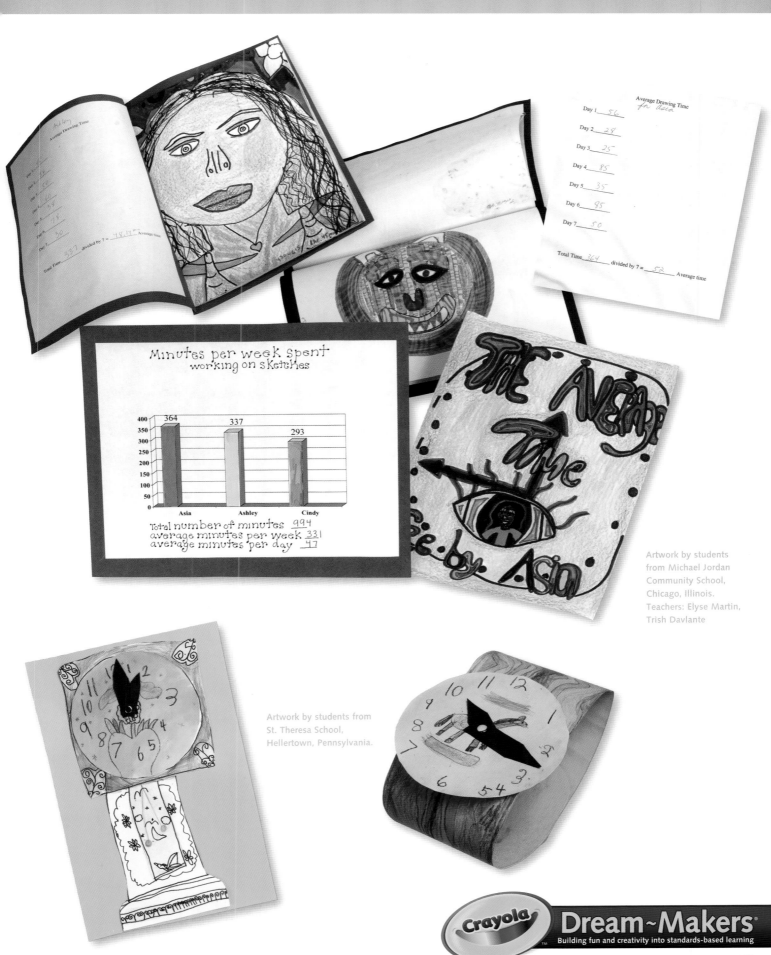

Average Drawing Time
for Asia

Day 1 _56_

Day 2 _28_

Day 3 _25_

Day 4 _85_

Day 5 _35_

Day 6 _95_

Day 7 _50_

Total Time _364_ divided by 7 = _52_ Average time

Minutes per week spent working on sketches

Total number of minutes _994_
average minutes per week _331_
average minutes per day _47_

Artwork by students from Michael Jordan Community School, Chicago, Illinois. Teachers: Elyse Martin, Trish Davlante

Artwork by students from St. Theresa School, Hellertown, Pennsylvania.

Crayola Dream~Makers
Building fun and creativity into standards-based learning

It's About Time...Average Time!

	K-2	3-4	5-6
Suggested Preparation and Discussion	Assemble a sample sketchbook. Display two clocks with movable hour and minute hands, and sample sketchbook. Show the clocks. Discuss how time is measured. How long is a second, minute, half hour, hour? Ask children to name activities that take different amounts of time to do, such as brushing teeth or traveling to school. Use clocks to show start and finish times for several typical activities. Ask students how long they think it will take them to carefully create similar sketchbooks (this is not a race). Record estimates. Set a clock at the start time. Create sketchbooks: Demonstrate how to sandwich seven sheets of copy paper inside folded drawing paper. Staple along spine. Set a second clock to show the finish time. Together calculate how long it took. Compare actual time to estimates.	Discuss the subject of graffiti. Have students share where they have seen graffiti. How long does it take to create graffiti? Explain that fine artists take time and practice drawing in sketchbooks to prepare for creating larger works such as mural paintings. Share examples of large outdoor murals such as those created by the Philadelphia Mural Arts Program. With students, create sketchbooks. Sandwich seven sheets of white paper inside folded drawing paper. Staple along spine. Ask students how long they think it will take them to create seven detailed drawings of the things they see around them (there is no rush)? What do they think will be the average time per drawing? Ask each student to record this estimate on the back cover of his/her sketchbook. Explain how to calculate an average. Tell students that, although each sketch will take a different amount of time, after they are finished they will be able to calculate the average time per sketch. Show how to calculate an average by asking how many days last week each student brought lunch or did some other similar, variable task. Tally the results; divide the total by the number of students in the class. Create a bar graph poster to illustrate how students will chart their drawing times.	

Crayola® Supplies
- Colored Pencils
- Crayons
- Markers

Other Materials
- Calculators
- Clock(s)
- Copy paper
- Staplers and staples
- Stopwatch(es) (optional)
- White drawing paper (12- x 18-inch)

Process: Session 1 20-30 min.

Design cover

1. Children write the word "TIME" on the covers of their sketchbooks. Decorate the covers with shapes and patterns around the letters.
2. Explain that each day students will complete a different task at home or school. Children draw a picture of each task in their sketchbooks and write how many minutes each task took.

Design cover

1. Students draw decorative letters to create titles for their sketchbooks. Add interest by including increasingly more elaborate shapes, colors, and patterns.
2. Explain to students that they will create detailed drawings of objects they see. They are to record the time in minutes that it takes to do each daily drawing in small data blocks in one corner of each of seven pages: "START," "FINISH," and "ELAPSED TIME." Students calculate elapsed time daily or at the end of their research.

Process: Sessions 2 20-30 min.

Collect data over 7 days

3. Each day children measure how long it takes to do activities such as watch ice cream melt, walk around the entire school together, or draw a detailed self-portrait. They record an estimate before actually timing each task. Evaluate estimates.

Collect data over 7 days

3. Review the assignment each day. Students share their sketches with classmates. Talk about how long it took to create each one.

Czech Clock
Photo by R. De Long

	K-2	3-4	5-6

Process: Session 3 20-30 min.

K-2	3-4
Sort and analyze data	**Sort, evaluate, and display data**
4. Students review their sketchbooks to find the tasks that took the most and least time. List all the tasks in order according to times.	4. Students calculate the total time it took for each of them to create all seven drawings.
5. Share sketchbook drawings and compare elapsed times for various students doing similar tasks.	5. Students divide the sum by seven to find the average (arithmetic mean) time that drawings were made for one week.
6. Show students how to create bar graphs using their data. Encourage them to use a different color for each activity.	6. Share drawings and findings. Compare and graph data, individually and as a class. Analyze findings.
	7. Advanced students perform more sophisticated calculations with the data, such as comparing the range of time differences or calculating the percentage of total time each drawing took. Use class time data to calculate mean, median, and mode.
	8. Challenge students to turn time calculated in minutes into fractional and decimal expressions of parts of an hour. Then calculate averages using these figures.

Assessment

K-2	3-4
• Review student sketchbooks to check for accurate recording of tasks and time measurements.	• Students work in pairs to check each other's calculations with a calculator. • Compare and discuss bar graphs.

• Ask students to reflect on this lesson and write a DREAM statement to summarize the most important things they learned.

Extensions

K-2	3-4	5-6
Create a time survey with children to find out how families enjoy time together and how much time they spend doing their favorite activities. Have children generate survey questions and record data at home. Create dioramas showing how each family spends time together. See Family Food Favorites on Crayola.com for creative inspiration.	Investigate how things change over hours, days, and months. Document changes with drawings and mathematical data in layered tab books. See the How Time Flies Lesson Plan on Crayola.com for directions.	Students with strong mathematical backgrounds define and explain the terms *median* and *mode* to the class. Work together in small groups to have students determine the median and mode for the data collected on the sketchbook project. Discuss results.
Younger children and those who need more practice make paper plate clocks that have moveable hands attached with brass paper fasteners. Children use them to solve relevant time story problems.	Hold elapsed time showdowns! Students create clocks with moveable hands. One partner's clock is labeled "start time;" the other is "end time." Each clock can indicate a.m. or p.m. Partners stand back-to-back and record times on their clocks. Call out "showdown." Students turn to their partners and calculate the elapsed time between the clocks.	Challenge small groups of students to create elapsed-time game shows. Students identify problems related to calculating time, elapsed time, and average time as brainteasers for contestants. Hold a game show day.

	5-6
Children make a chart of their daily activities. Set the hands on a paper clock to indicate when they do these activities (wake up, go to school, eat lunch). Children draw pictures to illustrate the different activities.	Hold an obstacle course rally, much like a car rally. Students time each other in a series of challenges that they invent. Record individual data for each event. Total times to determine elapsed times for each student. Use data to calculate averages, means, modes, and medians for each event and the entire rally.

Swiss Clock
Photo by R. De Long

Purchasing Flower Power!

Objectives

Students assess the characteristics of their flower creations and those of their classmates as they recognize the artistic merits of creating individual flowers by hand and combining them into bouquets.

Students use place value and estimation to read, write, compare, and order decimals involving money, using play money to practice purchasing flowers within a budget.

Students create flowers using a multi-step batik-like technique.

Multiple Intelligences

Interpersonal	Naturalist
Logical-mathematical	

National Standards

Visual Arts Standard #5	Mathematics Standard
Reflects upon and assesses the characteristics and merits of their work and the work of others	*Grades K-2* ***Algebra*** Use mathematical modes to represent and understand quantitative relationships *Grades K-6* ***Number and Operations*** Compute fluently and make reasonable estimates ***Problem Solving*** Solve problems that arise in mathematics and in other contexts

Background Information

Most flowers and plants sold in the United States are grown locally. Some, however, come from great distances. Florists get a variety of plant materials from wholesalers, who obtain them from huge international auctions. The largest flower auction in the world is held in Aalsmeer, Holland. Imagine an auction building that covers 160 acres with complex, computerized moving and tracking systems for their fragile wares. About 14 million flowers are auctioned every day in Aalsmeer—that's 3 billion flowers a year! Blooms include colorful carnations, chrysanthemums, freesia, lilacs, and roses. Most of these flowers are shipped to other countries.

Your favorite, fragrant flower in a Mother's Day bouquet or wedding arrangement may have been grown in Bulgaria, auctioned in Holland, flown by jet across the ocean, and then trucked to your hometown.

Concept List

Use this list to explore new vocabulary, create idea webs, or brainstorm related subjects.

10% off
25% reduction
30% less
Auctioneer
Banker
Botanist
Bouquets
Careers
Discount calculations
Financial planner
Florist
Horticulturist
Imported
Individual items
Local
Mandalas
Manufacturer
Marketer/advertiser
Multiples

Production costs
Radial design
Repetition, rhythm, & pattern
Retailer
Rose windows
Seasonal
Stock broker
Vendor

Resources

Flowers by David Burnie
Bright illustrations and photographs with detailed text. Presents botany in a fun framework. Older students are intrigued by information, while younger students are inspired by colorful images.

The Reason for a Flower by Ruth Heller
Rich illustrations present the many functions of flowers. Text is just right for lessons on basic botany. Excellent resource for all grade levels.

Flower Market
Arles, France
Photo by J. McCracken

Radial design
in a tile design.

The Creation, Rose Window
Washington National Cathedral
Washington, D.C.
Photo by J. McCracken

Artwork by students from
PS 132K, Brooklyn, New York.
Teacher: Charlotte Ka

Artwork by students from
Trinity Kids Club,
Trinity Wesleyan Church,
Allentown, Pennsylvania.
Teacher: Alison Panik

Crayola® Dream~Makers®
Building fun and creativity into standards-based learning

Purchasing Flower Power!

	K-2	3-4	5-6
Suggested Preparation and Discussion	Display pictures of flower arrangements that contain more than three flowers. Display other artifacts that illustrate radial design, such as photographs of rose window and mandala designs and close-up views of flowers. Discuss how flowers are bought and sold. Talk about how flowers could be purchased by the stem or in bouquets. Ask children what they know about how flowers are grown, priced, shipped, and sold. Ask students whether they think it is more expensive to purchase a whole bouquet or to buy individual stems to make your own bouquet. Find out! Create some unusual blossoms following the steps here to use in display, discussions, and demonstrations.		
	Look closely at illustrations and photographs of flowers that clearly demonstrate radial design. Ask children what shapes they notice. Place strings across the photo to show the symmetry of the flower in each "pie slice."	Lead children to develop a plan to research and compare the real costs of creating a bouquet within a budget. Where could they go to find out? With student assistance, create simple paper money—$1, $5, $10, and $20 bills as well as coins. Identify samples of radial design found in nature and art.	
	Explain that students will "manufacture and sell" flowers within a budget. After creating several single-stem flowers that will demonstrate radial design, they price their flower stems individually. With those flowers, they will put together beautiful bouquets, but the cost of the entire bouquet may not exceed the assigned budget!		
Crayola® Supplies	• Colored Pencils • Fabric Crayons • Glitter Glue • Scissors • Washable Markers		
Other Materials	• Coffee filters • Green floral tape • Hole punch • Iron (adult use only) • Oak tag • Paper towels • Recycled newspaper • Ribbon or yarn • Sealable plastic bags • White paper		
Set-up/Tips	• Use play money coins. Or ask parents to provide real coins in sealable plastic bags labeled with each child's name.		
	• Cover art surfaces with newspaper. • Place newspaper under coffee filters for better control during coloring and ironing. Show children how to apply firm pressure when coloring coffee filters with fabric crayons to achieve the best color results. • Store each child's coffee filter flowers in a large sealable plastic bag labeled with the child's name between sessions. • Enlist parent volunteers to iron coffee filters.		
Process: Session 1 30-45 min. (plus ironing)	**Create flower blossom radial designs** 1. Demonstrate how to fold a coffee filter in halves, quarters, and then in eighths by folding in half again, again, and again. 2. Unfold and press the coffee filter flat. Draw radial designs on several coffee filters with fabric crayons, adding similar lines, shapes, and colors in each section. Leave some sections plain. 3. AN ADULT heat-sets the crayon. Place plain paper on newspaper. Lay filter on the paper. Cover with a second sheet of paper. AN ADULT irons the filter with a hot iron in a well-ventilated area. Press the design with slow steady pressure, moving from area to area slowly for 1 to 2 minutes. Colors will "bleed" a bit like batik. Cool.		
Process: Session 2 20-30 min.	**Add marker colors** 4. Fold the ironed coffee filters several times. 5. Press washable marker nibs against the folded filter and hold in position so the filter absorbs color through all layers. Unfold. 6. Dampen paper towels. Gently press on coffee filters to dampen them, diffusing marker color for added effects. Air-dry filters.		
Process: Session 3 15-20 min.	**Add glitter glue** 7. Decorate blossom centers and edges with glitter glue. Outline interesting parts to make them stand out. Air-dry the filters.		

	K-2	3-4	5-6

**Process:
Session 4
30-40 min.**

Create stems

8. Gather the finished blossom into a cone. Press the pointed end flat against the top of a colored pencil barrel.

9. Wrap floral tape around the point of the filter and over the pencil to attach blossom to pencil (see diagram).

Make price tags

10. Cut 1- x 2-inch rectangles of oak tag to create price tags. Punch a hole in one end of tag and insert ribbon or yarn.

11. Provide ability-appropriate direction to students regarding pricing. (For example, younger students might price flowers in 5¢ increments—5¢, 10¢—while older students use larger dollar and cent amounts.) Students decide on the price of each of their flower stems and write the prices on the tags using decimal dollar notation ($.79) on one side and cents notation (79¢) on the other. Encourage children to take into account the work that went into creating each individual flower and the uniqueness of each bloom.

12. Create decorative borders on both sides of the price tags. Tie price tags to flower stems.

Assessment

K-2	3-4	5-6
• Arrange flowers in containers to create a flower market display. Children sort flowers according to a variety of physical characteristics. • Provide plastic coins for children to use to "purchase" single stems and different combinations of two or more stems. Observe children's abilities to calculate and count coins.	• Set a predetermined budget. Teams of students calculate the cost of buying several flowers while staying within their budget. How many combinations can they create within their budget? • Set up a flower market and provide play money for students to use to "pay" for different bouquets. Observe calculation and problem-solving skills.	• Arrange flowers in a flower market display. Students work in pairs to choose, calculate, and "purchase" different combinations of flowers, using bills and coins. Observe students' abilities to calculate cost, count money, give change, and use problem-solving skills to exchange one flower for another to get the most for their budgets.

• Ask students to reflect on this lesson and write a DREAM statement to summarize the most important things they learned.

Extensions

K-2	3-4	5-6
Very young children and those with some disabilities may be most successful in decorating blossoms only with washable markers and then spritzing them with water. They may also need assistance with wrapping the floral tape. At the end of the unit, create vases to display flowers in the school. See Very Versatile Vases on Crayola.com for a unique technique. Tip: Place a rock at the bottom to prevent toppling. Grow flowers from seeds. Price and sell them at a school event.	Depending on the time of year, take the artistic flower experiences into the real world. In winter, force blooms from dormant flowering trees and shrubs (such as azaleas and dogwoods). In spring, plant and grow marigolds from seeds. In fall, extract natural dyes from colorful flowers and leaves. Place fabric over flowers and leaves and pound with a mallet.	Research plant breeding. Explore different kinds of cut flowers to see variations in color, size, fragrance, and petal shape. Discuss why floriculturists and geneticists might want to create new and different kinds of flowers. Talk about intellectual property and the breeder's bill of rights. Why does the price of flowers vary so much? Gifted students could investigate the cost of seeds/cuttings, greenhouse/field environments, growing seasons, shipping, and various other factors that play a role in the price of flowers.

Radial design in a hibiscus flower.

How to fasten paper blossom to pencil stem

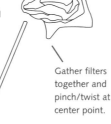

Gather filters together and pinch/twist at center point.

Tightly wrap floral tape to join blossom to pencil stem.

Wrap until blossom is secure on stem.

Crayola **Dream~Makers**
Building fun and creativity into standards-based learning

Personal Math Motto Banners

Objectives

Students write algebraic equations to show how lines are used to create plane figures, and how plane figures are used to create the illusion of three-dimensional space figures.

Students connect similarities and differences between visual arts and mathematics by analyzing and applying the equations in 2-D and 3-D figures.

Students develop an appropriate problem-solving plan, and then draw pictures to arrange lines, shapes, colors, and textures to create 3-D illusions on banners.

Students identify mottos that relate to mathematical problem solving or geometric proofs.

Multiple Intelligences

Intrapersonal
Linguistic
Logical-mathematical
Spatial

What Does It Mean?

Contour drawing: drawing that focuses on edges and three-dimensional outlines of objects, folds, or patterns using line without shading

Trompe l'Oeil: artwork that is portrayed realistically so that people think they are looking at something real; visual illusion such that 2-D paintings appear to be 3-D

National Standards

Visual Arts Standard #6 Makes connections between visual arts and other disciplines	**Mathematics Standards** *Algebra* Represent and analyze mathematical situations and structures using algebraic symbols *Reasoning and Proof* Select and use various types of reasoning and methods of proof

Background Information

Some artists are so skillful at creating illusions that they fool the viewer into thinking they see three-dimensional objects in real space even though the art is only two-dimensional. One method of illusion painting is called Trompe l'Oeil, which means "fool the eye." Because these kinds of paintings are on flat (two-dimensional) surfaces, it takes much observation, planning, and even mathematical skill to create these illusions. Throughout history, artists have used various devices to help them duplicate the look of three-dimensional objects, or to create the illusion that one object is close and another very far away.

Resources

A Trick of the Eye: Trompe l'Oeil Masterpieces by Eckhard Hollman and Jurgen Tesch
Explores five centuries of Trompe l'Oeil: optical illusion, hyperrealism, and visual puns. Identifies tricks artists use to manipulate visual perception. Something for all ages.

Grandfather Tang's Story by Ann Tompert
Ages 6 through 9 enjoy this tale of two shape changers told by a Chinese grandfather. He illustrates the story by shifting tangrams into different shapes. Includes a tangram pattern.

Seeing Double by J. Richard Block
Use age-appropriate examples from this collection of more than 200 illustrations to demonstrate how shapes can be arranged to give impressions of more than one idea.

Vocabulary List

Use this list to explore new vocabulary, create idea webs, or brainstorm related subjects.

- Algebra terms

  Equation
  Unknown
  Variable

- Design with shapes

  Inversions/ mirror images
  Patterns
  Symmetry
  Tessellations

- Illusions

  Optical
    After-images
    Pictographic ambiguity
  Famous artists
    Josef Albers
    M.C. Escher
    Raphael
    Victor Vasarely
  Magic

- Mottos

  Guiding principal, goal, or ideal
  Sentence, phrase, or word
  Spirit, character, or purpose of a
    person or group

- Three-dimensional (3-D) art

  Contour drawings
  Depth
  Form
  Shadow
  Volume

**Japanese Textile
Banner**
2001
Unknown artisan
Paint on dyed silk
15" x 31"
Kyoto, Japan
Private Collection.

Building fun and creativity into standards-based learning

Personal Math Motto Banners

K-2	3-4	5-6

Suggested Preparation and Discussion

Post several quotations related to mathematics or problem solving, such as Carl Sandburg's "Arithmetic is where numbers fly like pigeons in and out of your head." Read the quotations aloud and ask students to explain what they think they mean.

Display pictures of quilt designs that create 3-D illusions through the juxtaposition of simple light- and dark-colored shapes.

Create a bulletin board showing the "recipe" or equation for a shape. Demonstrate how two horizontal lines and two vertical lines combine to create a square.

With students, make a matching game using recycled household items shaped as a cone, cube, cylinder, pyramid, plastic egg, sphere, and rectangular prism. Write the names of the shapes on cards to match the objects.

Start a bulletin board showing the equation:

(A+B)+(A+B)=C

(horizontal line + vertical line) + (horizontal line + vertical line) = square. Invite students to create several more equation "recipes" for a variety of regular plane figures (rectangle, triangle, hexagon). More advanced students add irregular figures.

With students, create a poster with line drawings illustrating 3-D figures: cone, cube, cylinder, pyramid, egg form, sphere, and rectangular prism. Write names of forms on separate pieces of paper. Children match names of figures to forms. Expand the activity to include a set of small cards with names of plane figures and a set of small number cards. Challenge students to identify the plane figures required to create each space figure and how many of each are needed to make the figures.

Children use colored craft sticks, yarn, and rubber bands to analyze how lines are used to create plane figures (squares, circles, rectangles, triangles). Ask children to explain what kinds of lines are needed to create each shape.

Use paper shapes to analyze how plane figures are used to create 3-D space figures. Explore how tangrams can be arranged to create the illusion of 3-D figures on a flat surface. Discuss how combined shapes create identifiable objects such as figures, animals, and plants.

Look at examples of Trompe l'Oeil, optical illusions, and geometric art. Invite students to think about combinations of lines that create shapes.

Crayola® Supplies

• Colored Pencils • Fabric Crayons • Fabric Markers • Glitter Glue • School Glue • Scissors

Other Materials

• Construction paper • Fine-grade sandpaper sheets (optional) • Freezer paper (optional)
• Iron (for adult use only, optional) • Newsprint • White cotton fabric • White paper • Yarn or ribbon

Set-up/Tips

• Ask parent volunteers to measure and cut a clean, white cotton sheet into 18- x 24-inch pieces, one for each child.

• Cover drawing surface with plain newsprint.

• For more intense fabric crayon colors, place fabric on top of a very fine grade of sandpaper before decorating. Hold in place with masking tape as needed. Press hard and lay down a thick layer of crayon. Fabric crayon colors look much brighter when they are heat set.

• To stabilize fabric for decorating with either markers or crayons, ask adult volunteers to iron freezer paper on the back.

• Adults heat-set the fabric crayon or marker color designs according to package directions (optional).

Japanese Textile Banner
2001
Unknown artisan
Paint on silk brocade
15" x 39 1/4"
Kyoto, Japan
Private Collection.

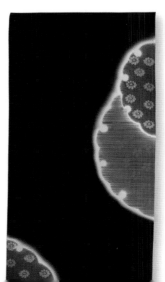

Japanese Textile Banner
2001
Unknown artisan
Paint on silk brocade
15" x 25 1/2"
Kyoto, Japan
Private Collection.

	K-2	3-4	5-6

Process: Session 1 20-30 min.

Sketch 2-D and 3-D designs

1. On paper, students plan their own personal illusion illustrations, one with plane figures and one with space figures. The student art samples pictured were made with two large squares, one above the other. Place 2-D plane figures in the top and 3-D figures in the bottom square.

Process: Session 2 30-40 min.

Create fabric designs

2. Use fabric crayons or fabric markers to draw the planned illustrations on fabric. Be sure to leave a 1 1/2-inch border at the top for hanging and a 3-inch space to separate the shapes.

Process: Session 3 20-30 min.

Choose mottos

3. Brainstorm encouraging and/or humorous words, phrases, and sentences about problem solving and math.

4. Children choose mottos that stand out for them. Write mottos on banners.

Research mottos

3. Children research pertinent quotations about math and problem-solving or geometric proofs. Or they create their own inspirational math mottos.

4. Write chosen mottos on banners.

Process: Session 4 15-20 min.

Embellish designs

5. If the designs are to be heat set, an adult does this before proceeding.

6. Embellish designs with glitter glue. Air-dry the glue.

Process: Session 5 10-15 min.

Prepare banner for display

7. Roll construction paper. Glue the end to form a cylinder. Hold in place until air-dry.

8. Apply glue to back of top 1-inch border of fabric. Place paper cylinder onto the glued border and roll. Air-dry the glue.

9. Cut ribbon or yarn into 3-foot length. Thread through the cylinder and tie closed to hang.

Assessment

- On index cards, children write equations for some of the shapes they created in their designs. Talk with students about the designs and their equations to assess learning.
- Do banners include a variety of shapes?

- Students write equations for the lines needed to create each plane figure, the shapes needed to create each space figure, and the figures needed to create illusions in their designs. Ask students to exchange papers to check equations.
- Do the images on the students' banners show an understanding of how lines and colors can be manipulated to create visual illusions?

- Are the mottos chosen for the banners pertinent and spelled properly?
- Ask students to reflect on this lesson and write a DREAM statement to summarize the most important things they learned. Write or print statements on labels to attach to the back of each student's banner.

Extensions

Print out the Eye Illusions activity page from Crayola.com. Discuss each illusion, then challenge children to create their own.

Cut tangram pieces from recycled file folders for younger children and those with some learning disabilities to manipulate into animal shapes. After shapes are defined, students add texture and color to clarify the image.

Share the book *Hello, Red Fox* by Eric Carle with the class. Talk about how illusions can be created through the use of complementary colors.

Challenge students to invent new optical illusions, adding movement to the equation. Provide a variety of art materials, such as acetate sheets, recycled file folders, straws, and brass fasteners for students to experiment with spinning, flipping, and bending images. Encourage students to think of their own ideas and go to Crayola.com for inspirational crafts, such as Flash a Neon Mini-Sign, Geometric Optic Spinner, and Optical Delusion.

Student research groups investigate the work of famous illusionists and explain special techniques they used to create their illusions.

Invite an ophthalmologist to speak to the class about how movies create an illusion of movement.

Challenge students with strong spatial awareness to create tessellations.

Animals: A Brood, a Clutter, a Drift, and More!

Objectives

Students recognize various materials, techniques and processes, and can describe and use these to communicate ideas, experiences, and number stories to elicit viewer response.

Students (K-2) count with understanding, recognize "how many" in sets of objects, and compare sizes of those sets.

Students (3-4) identify and build three-dimensional objects from two-dimensional representations of that object.

Students (5-6) use geometric models to represent and explain algebraic relationships among the sets depicted.

Multiple Intelligences

Interpersonal	Naturalist
Linguistic	Spatial
Logical-mathematical	

National Standards

Visual Arts Standard #3 Chooses and evaluates a range of subject matter, symbol, and ideas	**Mathematics Standards** ***Number and Operations*** Understand numbers, ways of representing numbers, relationships among numbers, and number systems ***Problem Solving*** Build new mathematical knowledge through problem solving ***Connections*** Recognize and apply mathematics in contexts outside of mathematics

Background Information

Why are groups of animals called different names? Some choices seem obvious, such as a colony of bats or ants, or a herd of deer or cattle. Other group names may be romantic or even mysterious, such as these unusual animal group names:

- a dole of doves
- a business of ferrets
- a knot of frogs
- a horde of hamsters
- a charm of hummingbirds
- a parliament of owls
- a gang of weasels
- a murder of crows

A group of birds of any species is usually called a flock. Crows, with their sinister associations, may have earned their group name by their association with melodrama, such as the work of Edgar Allen Poe.

Lexicographers suggest that group names of animals have their roots in animal behaviors. Names such as a *pride of lions* or a *gaggle of geese* seem to support that theory. But what about hamsters and ferrets?

Resources

A Crash of Rhinos, a Party of Jays: The Wacky Ways We Name Animal Groups by Diane Swanson and Mariko Ando Spencer
A whimsical introduction to animal groups appropriate for all ages. Comic illustrations for each animal and group name. Counting opportunity for early elementary classes.

Animals: Pictures and Words by Carolyn Jackson
More than 175 different animals featured in color photographs and illustrations that attract students of all ages. Older elementary children will be intrigued with facts about animal behavior.

Vocabulary List

Use this list to explore new vocabulary, create idea webs, or brainstorm related subjects.

Band (gorillas)
Bed (clams, oysters)
Brace (ducks)
Brood (chicks, hens)
Cast (hawks)
Clutter (cats)
Colony (ants)
Company (parrots)
Drift (hogs)
Flock (birds, sheep)
Gaggle (geese)
Gang (elk)
Herd (cattle, elephants)
Knot (toads)

Litter (kittens, pigs)
Murder (crows)
Muster (peacocks)
Pack (hounds, wolves)
Pod (seals, whales)
Pride (lions)
School (fish)
Skulk (foxes)
Sleuth (bears)
Swarm (bees)
Team (horses)
Troop (kangaroos)

Artwork by students from Mountain Plains School, Morris Plains, New Jersey. Teacher: Val Negra

group-Colony   webbed feet
birds
PENGUINS

A Nest of Snakes.

Artwork by students from
Mountain Plains School,
Morris Plains, New Jersey.
Teacher: Val Negra

Animals: A Brood, a Clutter, a Drift, and More!

	K-2	3-4	5-6
Suggested Preparation and Discussion	Display age-appropriate books and other pictures of groups of animals. With students, label them. Make a three-dimensional model depicting a set of one kind of animal.		
Crayola® Supplies	• Colored Pencils • Crayons • Model Magic® • School Glue • Scissors		
Other Materials	• Drawing paper • Modeling tools such as plastic dinner knives, craft sticks, and toothpicks • Velcro® tape • White paper		
			• Poster board
Set-up/Tips	• Work on a clean, dry surface. • Model Magic® compound fresh from the package sticks to itself. If the modeling material has dried, use glue to attach pieces.		
Process: Session 1 20-30 min.	**Choose and research an animal group** 1. Students each choose an animal from the photos displayed. 2. Students identify the animals' group names. 3. Students list facts they know about the animal selected, including habitat.	**Research animal groups** 1. Students research facts about one type of animal. 2. Students write a paragraph that includes facts they discovered. 3. Title the writing with the name that is given to the animal group.	**Research animal groups** 1. Teams of three or four students work together to select research facts about three or four different types of animals. 2. Compile a chart with columns for each animal. Title each column with the group name that corresponds to the animals. 3. List animal facts about each animal in each column.
		4. Create a diorama that includes 2-D drawings of the animal(s) researched. Draw animal features to accurately represent research facts. Depict the animal's natural habitat.	

Berks County cows
Photo by R. De Long

Zebra-head lamps
Photo by R. De Long

	K-2	3-4	5-6

Process: Session 2 45-50 min.

Create 3-D animal sets

4. Use a tennis ball amount of Model Magic compound to mold an animal body form. Use geometric forms such as spheres, cubes, cylinders, and rectangular prisms. Model, pinch and pull animal legs, necks, heads, tails, or other animal features to make a realistic animal.

5. Create a set of the same kind of animal. Use modeling tools to add texture and details. Make both adults and young.

6. Arrange animals on a Model Magic base representing their natural habitats. Air-dry models for 24 hours.

Process: Session 3 10-15 min.

Embellish animal sets

7. Decorate dried models with markers and/or watercolor. Air-dry paint.

Process: Session 4 20-30 min.

Count and compare set sizes	Compare 3-D with 2-D sets	Identify algebraic relationships
8. Label each set with the type of animal depicted.	8. Study the animal set models. Compare them with dioramas. Discuss correlations among 3-D forms and 2-D shapes.	8. Study the dioramas and animal models.
9. Study all the model animal sets. Count how many animals are in each set.	9. Calculate the number of geometric forms that were used to create the animal models. Which sets used the most different forms?	9. Identify algebraic relationships among the animal models, such as 1 (brood of 6) + 4 (brace of 5) = 20 birds
10. Identify sets that are equal in number. Compare sizes of sets using terminology such as *equal*, *less than*, and *more than*.		10. Students explain their math proofs to other teams.

Assessment

• Did each student depict one type of animal, show an accurate habitat, and label the set with its correct name? • How accurately did students count and compare the number of animals in each set?	• Are the features of the animals created in dioramas and sculpted sets accurate based on student research? • How descriptive were comparisons between 2-D and 3-D representations?	• Teams check each other's sets and math proofs. Do algebraic relationships compare groups, such as birds, four-legged animals, or water animals?

• Ask students to reflect on this lesson and write a DREAM statement to summarize the most important things they learned.

Extensions

Challenge students to compare and contrast the behaviors of animals. How do various animals relate to each other in terms of survival? Identify animals in the models that might have a predator-prey relationship.

Younger children and those with learning challenges may benefit from using common manipulatives such as table blocks to represent sets of animals before they create their own animal set models.

Write a step-by-step sequence of how to create a Model Magic animal set.

Students write descriptive paragraphs to explain how they arrived at their mathematical calculations.

Challenge students to explore the real relationships among animal groups in different habitats. Examine how the survival of each animal group depends on the survival of another.

Gifted students invent new species of animals by combining features from two or more animal species.

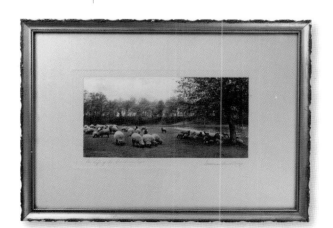

Sheep hand-colored photo Image
Artist: Wallace Nutting

Keeping Track of Time

Objectives

Students create a replica timepiece that reflects understanding of how a clock is heavily influenced by the visual arts in its design, while serving as a mathematical tool.

Students (K-2) develop a common referent to understand and practice how time is measured.

Students (3-4) select and apply appropriate standard units to estimate, measure, and compare the time it takes to conduct simple activities.

Students (5-6) recognize international time zones and the relationships among time units as they are converted from one to another within the system.

Multiple Intelligences

Interpersonal	Logical-mathematical

National Standards

Visual Arts Standard #1 Understands and applies media, techniques, and processes **Visual Arts Standard #4** Understands the visual arts in relation to history and cultures	**Mathematics Standards** ***Data Analysis and Probability*** Formulate questions that can be addressed with data and collect, organize, and display relevant data to answer them ***Measurement*** Understand measurable attributes of objects and the units, systems, and processes of measurement ***Problem Solving*** Apply and adapt a variety of appropriate strategies to solve problems ***Representation*** Create and use representations to organize, record, and communicate mathematical ideas

Background Information

People have come up with methods for measuring time apparently as long as history has been recorded. Ancient sundials were round disks marked with hours much like today's clocks. An upright structure cast a shadow on the disk on sunny days. While sundials were relatively efficient and evolved over several thousand years, they had limited use in cloudy weather.

The hourglass was invented to solve this challenge. An hourglass is formed by two round glass bulbs, one above the other, connected by a short, narrow neck. When the hourglass is turned over, sand flows slowly from the upper glass bulb into the lower one. The amount of sand, and the width of the neck, determine how long it takes for the sand to completely empty into the lower bulb.

In the 1300s, the first mechanical clocks were invented. Some were wound by springs, while swinging pendulums drove others. Inventors continued working to create clocks that were more and more accurate, with innovations including gears and wheels. By the early 1800s, mass-production of identical clock parts made it possible for almost everyone to own a timepiece.

Clock innovations continue. Digital and wireless clocks, such those that pick up radio waves to assure the correct time, are common. Chemistry contributed to the invention of the atomic clock, which tells time to almost perfect accuracy using a specific atom.

Resources

Clocks & More Clocks by Pat Hutchins
A fun introduction to telling time for younger students. Also offers a problem-solving situation for older students exploring the measurement of time.

Telling Time: How to Tell Time on Digital and Analog Clocks! by Jules Older & Megan Halsey
Clearly explains concepts of time, including the measurement of when something happens as well as how long something takes place. Good choice to introduce time and review concepts.

The Story of Clocks & Calendars by Betsy & Giulio Maestro
Details about the history of timekeeping complete with color photos and illustrations. For students in grade 3 and above.

Vocabulary List

Use this list to explore new vocabulary, create idea webs, or brainstorm related subjects.

- Measuring time

Units	Tools	Components of an analog clock
Century	Alarm clock	Bells
Day	Analog clock	Case
Decade	Atomic clock	Chimes
Hour	Calendar	Face
Minute	Cuckoo clock	Gears
Second	Digital clock	Hour hand
Week	Egg timer	Minute hand
Year	Hourglass	Numerals
	Pendulum (grandfather) clock	Pendulums
		Second hand
	Pocket watch	Springs
	Stopwatch	
	Sundial	
	Wristwatch	

- Art elements and principles

Balance	Pattern	Texture
Crayon resist	Proportion	Unity
Line	Shape	

Artwork created by students from
St. Theresa School,
Hellertown, Pennsylvania.

Artwork created by students from
Mount Propsect Elementary School,
Basking Ridge, New Jersey.
Teacher: Susan Bivona

	K-2	3-4	5-6
Suggested Preparation and Discussion	Display images and examples of different types of clocks. Talk about similarities and differences between historic and contemporary clocks. Discuss how time keeping changed over the years. Design an unusual, even humorous, timepiece to inspire student creativity. Note art elements used on the different clocks on display. Challenge students to invent their own clocks using these elements. Introduce and reinforce time-telling skills on different types of clocks. Read books about time and its passage.		
		Discuss recipes that include cooking times (such as "Bake for 45 minutes"). Read time schedules for public transportation. Invent and solve problems using these charts.	With students, chart times from at least three different time zones based on Coordinated Universal Time (UTC) also known as Greenwich Mean Time (GMT)/Zulu.
Crayola® Supplies	• Colored Pencils • Crayons • Glue Sticks • Markers • Paint Brushes • Scissors • Watercolors		
Other Materials	• Brads • Compasses (optional) • Construction paper • Paper towels • Recycled file folders • Recycled newspaper • Water containers • White paper		
Set-up/Tips	• Provide tools for drawing round faces such as compasses, clean plastic lids, recycled CDs, or paper plates. Demonstrate their use as needed. • Demonstrate how to press hard with crayons for best results with crayon resist. • Cover painting area with newspaper.		

Process: Session 1 45-50 min.

Draw a clock case

1. Students plan their clocks. Choose the size and shape of the clock box. Decide whether the clock will have hands, be digital, or use some other way to show time. Students must be able to change minutes and hours.

2. Draw imaginative clock cases using 2-D art elements (line, shape, color, texture). Glue paper together for large clocks, such as grandfather clocks.

Process: Session 2 45-50 min.

Make a clock face

3. Trace circles on file folders or poster board. With crayon, mark 12 hours with numerals, Roman numerals, or even symbols! Decorate clock face with a unified, balanced design. Leave some areas plain.

4. Draw and color hour and minute hands. Cut them out.

Create the clock display

3. Design and decorate colorful crayon clocks on file folders or poster board. Be creative with the design of clock hands, numeral fonts, and other elements.

4. Draw and color hour, minute, and second hands or other devices for tracking the passage of time. Cut them out as needed.

5. Paint the clock faces. Wax in the crayon resists the watercolor paint so the crayon color pops through. Air-dry the paint.

Sundial
South of France
Photo by J. McCracken

Town clock in Bern, Switzerland
Photo by R. De Long

	K-2	3-4	5-6
Process: Session 3 20-30 min.	**Assemble clocks** 6. Glue clock faces on the cases or background. 7. Attach any hands with a brad in the center of the face. Assemble other moving parts as needed.		
Process: Session 4 Grades K-2 20-30 min. Grades 3-6 45-50 min. or more	**Tell time** 8. Pair students to play telling time games appropriate to their abilities.. For example, role play "What am I doing when the clock shows…?" Set clock to a time. Give one hint. Using the hint and time of day, students write or illustrate the activity.	**Estimate, measure, and compare times** 8. Estimate the time it takes to do several simple tasks such as sharpen a pencil, read a recipe, or do homework. 9. Make a chart with three columns. Title the columns, Activity, Estimate, and Actual. 10. Note the time on the chart and the clock and then do the activity. 11. Move the hands on the clock to note the time when the activity was completed. 12. Calculate the amount of time it took to do the activity. How close was the estimate to the actual time?	**Use an international time-keeping system** 8. Teams of students research world time zones. Each student selects a city and positions the clock to match that city's time. 9. Calculate time differences (forward and backward) between the cities identified by members of the team. 10. Chart class information to show city name, country, and time zones represented.
Assessment	• Are numerals correctly arranged on clock faces? • Assess students' abilities to read and show times on clocks. • Determine student abilities to relate times to everyday activities.	• Observe students as they solve problems and figure out design challenges while creating their clocks. • Assess student ability to read recipes and/or schedules and show times on the clocks they created. • Review calculations of elapsed time for correctness.	• Check to see if students correctly calculate the differences in time between two cities. • Evaluate completeness and accuracy of chart.
	• Ask students to reflect on this lesson and write a DREAM statement to summarize the most important things they learned.		
Extensions	Involve several classes or even the whole school in this project! Encourage students to bring clocks from home (with parental permission) for a short-term display. Tally how many are collected per class, per grade, per type of clock, and other factors. Have each grade level create and display their clocks. Lead a variety of comparison activities using different categories at each grade level.		
	Create colorful clocks for extra practice using Crayola erasable products! See Clock Hands That Erase, a Lesson Plan on Crayola.com. Students use erasable markers to draw simple digital clocks on slick, small paper plates or individual white boards. Play matching games with digital and analog (face) clocks.	Find out more about the kinds of clocks used to tell time around the world. Create a display of clocks with a map indicating the regions of origin. Go to Crayola.com to see how to create a Floral Cuckoo Clock.	Research big clocks, such as Big Ben in London and the large clock on Parliament Hill in Ottawa. Find out how these clocks work, how they are set, and how math contributed to building these landmarks. Check out the Canada Parliament Hill coloring page on Crayola.com for an introduction.
		Challenge gifted students to create their own elapsed-time board games.	

Spin a Radial Design

Objectives

Students (K-2) name, classify, draw, compare, describe attributes, and investigate two-dimensional shapes in radial symmetry.

Students (3-4) precisely describe, classify, and understand relationships among radial designs.

Students (5-6) make and test conjectures about geometric properties and relationships and develop logical arguments to justify conclusions about spinners they make that include radial designs.

Students use radial design motifs as the basis for creating working spinners.

Multiple Intelligences

Bodily-kinesthetic
Logical-mathematical
Spatial

What Does It Mean?

Motif: a distinctive and recurring form, shape, figure, or other feature in a design

Radial symmetry: when objects or sections fan out in a regular pattern form a central point

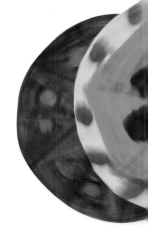

National Standards

Visual Arts Standard #3	Mathematics Standards
Chooses and evaluates a range of subject matter, symbols, and ideas	***Geometry*** Specify locations and describe spatial relationships using coordinate geometry and other representational systems
Visual Arts Standard #6 Makes connections between visual arts and other disciplines	***Communication*** Use the language of mathematics to express mathematical ideas precisely
	Connections Understand how mathematical ideas interconnect and build on one another to produce a coherent whole
	Representation Create and use representations to organize, record, and communicate mathematical ideas

Background Information

Invention of the kaleidoscope has been traced to a Scottish scientist, Sir David Brewster, who patented it in 1817. In the 1870s Charles Bush, from the United States, made improvements to the original design of the kaleidoscope and started a fad!

The word *kaleidoscope* is based on three Greek roots—*kalos* (beautiful), *eidos* (form), and *scope* (to see). Intersecting mirrors inside a kaleidoscope reflect beautiful repeated patterns formed by small objects such as pieces of colorful glass that rotate around a central point.

Resources

Hex Signs: Pennsylvania Dutch Barn Symbols & Their Meaning by Don Yoder & Thomas E. Graves
Color photographs display the use of radial symmetry in the folk art of hex signs. Useful for identifying line, shape, and colors seen in each repeated section of hex designs. Information about the meaning of each symbol. For students of all ages.

Kids Book of Kaleidoscopes by Carolyn Bennett & Jack Romig
Demonstrates how to build a simple kaleidoscope. For grades 3 and up. Illustrations and text explain light refraction and reflective symmetry concepts in a fun and friendly presentation. Created by a kaleidoscope designer.

Starfish by Lloyd G. Douglas
Introduce the concept of radial symmetry to younger students using the full color photographs of starfish. Close-up views of the detailed patterns on starfish arms will inspire identification of line, shape, and color that can carry over to children's designs.

Vocabulary List

Use this list to explore new vocabulary, create idea webs, or brainstorm related subjects.

- Terms

Axis	Line	Reflective
Balance	Midpoint	Shape
Circular	Mirror-image	Similar
Color	Motif	Symmetry
Fraction	Pattern	
Identical	Radial	

- Examples of radial symmetry

Anemone	Grapefruit half	Rose windows
Coral	Hex sign	Rosette designs
Flower	Hub cap	Starfish
	Jellyfish	
	Kaleidoscope	

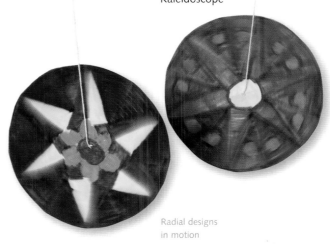

Radial designs in motion

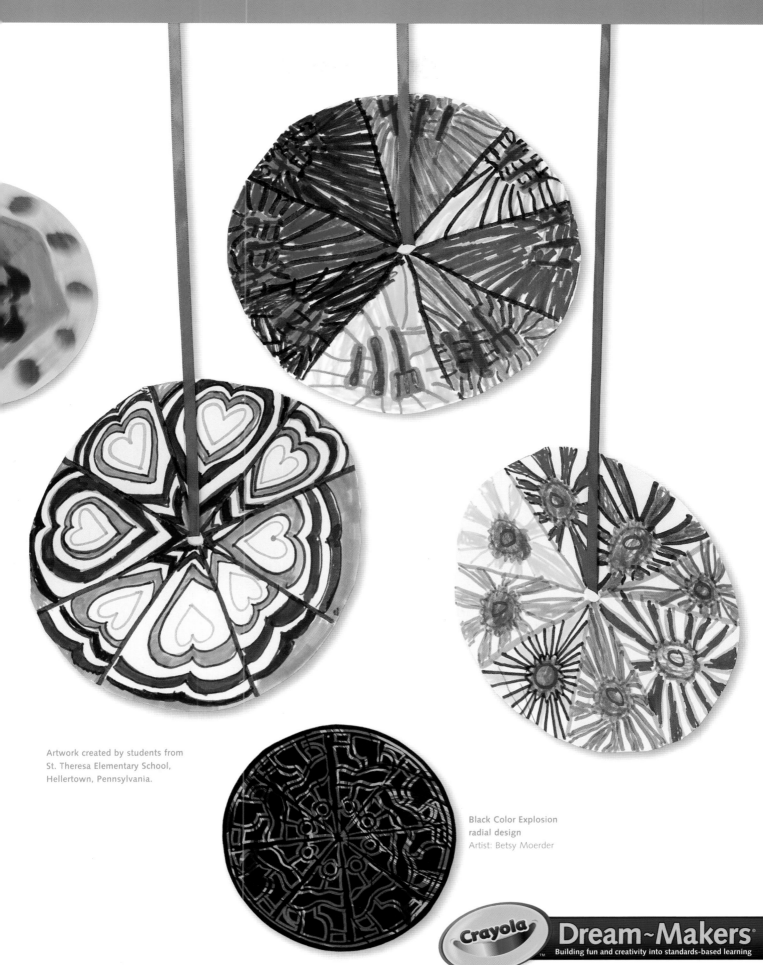

Artwork created by students from
St. Theresa Elementary School,
Hellertown, Pennsylvania.

Black Color Explosion
radial design
Artist: Betsy Moerder

Crayola

Dream~Makers®

Building fun and creativity into standards-based learning

Spin a Radial Design

	K-2	3-4	5-6
Suggested Preparation and Discussion	Display a variety of manufactured and natural objects that illustrate radial designs, such as clocks, flower blossoms, decorative plates, hubcaps, and kaleidoscopes. Introduce radial art from other cultures, such as Pennsylvania German hex signs, Aztec calendars, and Tibetan mandalas. Examine the symmetry in the objects. Calculate a symmetrical division of sections within each design. How many times is a motif in the symmetry repeated? Identify the shapes, lines, and colors in the repeated motif in each design. Photocopy a picture of a radial motif. Study the repeated motif. Cut apart the sections. Challenge students to reassemble the pieces. Create a sample spinner. Show students how to create and use the spinner.		
Crayola® Supplies	• Colored Pencils • Markers • School Glue • Scissors		
Other Materials	• Paper plates (small) • Recycled file folders • Rulers • White paper • Yard sticks or measuring tapes • Yarn or string		
Process: Session 1 20-30 min.	**Classify radial designs** 1. Students classify several samples of radial designs by line, shape, and color.	**Identify motifs** 1. Students select motifs for their radial designs. Motifs must include lines, shapes, and colors.	**Predict radial design attributes** 1. Students list factors that they think will prove that a design can be both radial and symmetrical while in motion.
Process: Session 2 20-30 min.	**Design motifs** 2. Trace around paper plates on paper to create circles. Cut out circles. Fold them into six equal pie-shaped sections. Cut along fold lines. 3. Sketch a motif in one section. Combine shapes, lines, and colors. Try different motifs in other sections. Choose a motif that is pleasing.		

Red Steel Tractor Wheels
Lancaster, Pennsylvania
Photo by J. McCracken

Interior of Dome, El Capitolio
de Puerto Rico
San Juan, Puerto Rico
Photo by Erica Simon-Brown

	K-2	3-4	5-6
Process: Session 3 45-60 min.	**Decorate spinners** 4. Trace around paper plates on recycled file folders. Cut out circles. Save scraps. 5. Use a ruler to divide the file folder circles into six sections the same size as the pie-shaped motif plan. 6. Follow the motif plan to decorate all six sections of the spinner.		
Process: Session 4 20-30 min.	**Assemble spinners** 7. Measure two 24-inch pieces of yarn. 8. Poke a hole in the center of the spinner with a pencil. Push about an inch of the yarn through the hole. 9. Put a dot of glue on a small folder scrap. Press it over the end of the yarn on the back of the spinner. Air-dry the glue.		
Process: Session 5 15-20 min.	**Spin designs** 10. Work in pairs to spin designs. One partner holds the top end of the yarn. The other partner turns the spinner round and round to twist the yarn. Let go to see the design spin!		**Analyze radial designs** 11. Students review their lists of factors that could prove that a design can be both radial and symmetrical while in motion. How many of these predictions are evident in the working spinners?
Assessment	• Students (K-2) accurately classify elements of symmetrical radial designs. Students (3-4) choose radial designs that include line, shape, and color. Students (5-6) orally justify their arguments that designs can be both radial and symmetrical when in motion. • Observe that spinners are assembled correctly and work properly. • Children describe their designs using math and art vocabulary (symmetry, balance, shapes, lines, and colors). • Ask students to reflect on this lesson and write a DREAM statement to summarize the most important things they learned.		
Extensions	Use the spinner plans to learn more about fractions. Cut each circle into sections. Place them on paper plates. Work in pairs to compare, add, and subtract fractions. Print Writing Fractions activity pages from Crayola.com for more practice. Experiment with how different shapes and designs have different lines of symmetry. Use unbreakable mirrors to produce multiple images.	Find out more about mandalas and the significance of symbols and objects that appear in them. Print mandala coloring pages from Crayola.com. Students construct mandalas to reflect their personalities and life experiences. See Cool Kaleidoscope Sun Catcher on Crayola.com for a unique way to bring light to these personal expressions. Hold a symmetry search! Challenge students to identify objects that exhibit different kinds of symmetry: reflective (mirror) symmetry, radial (rotational) symmetry, translation (sliding) symmetry, and gliding reflective (footprint) symmetry.	Gifted students research the history and science of kaleidoscopes. Find out how math is vital to their function. Build kaleidoscopes to experiment with visual perception. See the Color Kaleidoscopes lesson plan on Crayola.com. Measure the angles of each section radiating from the center of the spinner design. Experiment with designs using larger and smaller angles, keeping balance and radial symmetry in mind.

Parasailing Over the Caribbean
Palm Beach, Aruba
Photo by J. McCracken

Crayola Dream~Makers®
Building fun and creativity into standards-based learning

Balls: Classify, Roll, and Bounce

Objectives

Students (K-2) recognize, compare, sort, and classify balls according to attributes such as size, volume, weight, and decoration.

Students (3-4) use United States customary and metric units of measure as they experiment with, measure, and chart the distances that balls roll.

Students (5-6) select, and use United States customary and metric units to measure bounce height, bounce range, and graph data according to bounce characteristics.

Multiple Intelligences

Bodily-kinesthetic	Logical-mathematical
Interpersonal	Spatial

National Standards

Visual Arts Standard #1 Understands and applies media, techniques, and processes	**Mathematics Standards** **Measurement** Understand measurable attributes of objects and the units, systems, and processes of measurement Apply appropriate techniques, tools, and formulas to determine measurements **Connections** Recognize and apply mathematics in contexts outside of mathematics
	Science Standards *Grades K-4* Properties of objects and materials Position and motion of objects *Grades 5-6* Motions and forces Transfer of energy

Background Information

When a ball is dropped, gravity pulls it toward the ground. The ball gains energy from its downward motion. When the ball reaches the ground, that energy goes into changing the shape of the ball. Depending on how the ball is constructed—what material is used and other characteristics—the ball may flatten to the floor or bounce back up in the air.

The surface also affects how a ball bounces. A ball's speed is reduced significantly by its interaction with the ground. Two things affect the speed of the ball: the coefficient of restitution (COR) and the coefficient of friction (COF).

- How high a ball will bounce if dropped from a given height is the COR. A high COR surface gives a ball a higher bounce (the ball bounces off the surface almost as fast as it traveled to the surface). A low COR surface gives a ball a lower bounce (the ball bounces off the surface quite a bit slower than it traveled to the surface).

- The COF is the measurement of the frictional force of the ground surface on a ball. Friction slows down a ball. A high value of COF indicates a high frictional force on a ball—meaning that a ball's motion is stopped or slowed by material on the surface, such as carpet fibers.

Resources

Counting on Frank by Rod Clement
Get kids excited about calculating and measuring! Fun story about a boy and his dog, appropriate for all ages.

How Big Is a Foot? by Rolf Myller
A different approach to measuring puts the spotlight on uniform units of measure. Just right for younger students. Also presents compelling questions for older children.

Joey and Jet by James Yang
Younger students enjoy the adventures of a bouncing ball, a boy, and his dog.

Vocabulary List

Use this list to explore new vocabulary, create idea webs, or brainstorm related subjects.

Acceleration	Potential energy
Ball	Predict
Bounce	Shape
Compare	Speed
Energy	Sphere
Evaluate	Surface
Experiment	Texture
Form	Velocity
Fraction	
Friction	
Graph	
Gravity	
Height	
Kinetic energy	
Mass	
Material	
Measure	

How HIGH WILL IT BOUNCE?

34
33
32
31
30
29
28
27
26
25
24
23
22
21
20
19
18
17
16
15

THUD

Artwork created by students
from Freeman Elementary School,
Phillipsburg, New Jersey.
Teacher: Kathy Prichard

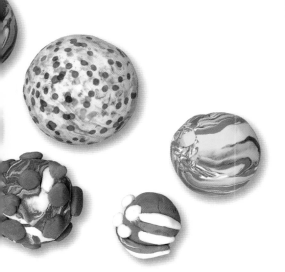

Balls: Classify, Roll, and Bounce

	K-2	3-4	5-6
Suggested Preparation and Discussion	Ask children to name spherical objects. What is the difference between a sphere and a circle? What happens when you view a sphere from different directions? What stays the same? Display balls and spheres in a variety of sizes, materials, textures, and weights, such as those shown here. Create several Model Magic® ball examples. Encourage children to handle and (if possible) roll and bounce them. Observe closely. Classifying, rolling, and bouncing balls can be fun and exciting! Provide time and space (preferably outdoors or in a gym) to safely compare, roll, and bounce sports balls (inflated and flat), as well as balls of yarn, snowballs, and other nontraditional spheres. Experience firsthand the physics of rolling, bouncing, and kinetic energy! Demonstrate sculpting techniques such as these: • Add washable marker color to white Model Magic compound. Blend for a marbleized effect. Knead more to create a solid color. • Wrap the compound around an object, such as a small rubber ball or bead. Roll between palms to smooth. • Poke indentations into the ball with a finger or modeling tool. • Wrap thin Model Magic rolls around a rubber ball or other object. Provide opportunities for students to use standard and nonstandard measuring tools.		
Crayola® Supplies	• Markers • Model Magic® • Scissors		
			• Paint Brushes • Tempera Paint
Other Materials	• Craft paper • Measuring tools (U.S. customary and metric) • Modeling tools such as plastic dinner knives, craft sticks, and toothpicks • Paper roll • Recycled boxes • White paper • Optional for ball construction: beads, bells, buttons, foil, Silly Putty®, small balls		
			• Masking tape • Optional for bounce chambers: cork sheets, felt, hard tiles, metal buckets, plastic containers • Recycled boxes • Recycled newspaper
Set-up/Tips	• Ask families to help gather beads, ribbon, string, and other items that can be used to create unique Model Magic balls and boxes that can be used as bounce chambers. • To increase bounce-ability variables, choose different surfaces for the bottom of bounce chambers such as hard plastic mats or soft bubble wrap or packing foam.		
Process: Session 1 30-50 min.	**Create balls** 1. Encourage students to use their imaginations to make various size balls. Make each ball unique by embedding assorted materials into the Model Magic compound. Air-dry the balls for at least 24 hours.		
Process: Session 2 30-min.	**Observe ball attributes** 2. Students observe all of the balls they created. 3. Children identify and orally describe ball attributes such as color, size, shape, decoration, and weight.	**Select units of measure** 2. Review U.S. customary and metric units of measure. 3. In teams of three of four, vote on which unit of measure to use for the "rolling balls" experiment.	**Select units of measure** 2. Review U.S. customary and metric units of measure. 3. In teams of three of four, vote on which unit of measure to use for the bounce experiments.

Variety of decorative spheres
Artist unknown
Private Collection.

	K-2	3-4	5-6
Process: Session 3 30-50 min.	**Create team charts** 4. In teams, create a chart on which to record ball attributes. Choose a team recorder. 5. Write headings in block letters and decorate the chart.	**Create rolling course and result charts** 4. On craft paper, teams create courses for measuring the lengths their balls roll. 5. Teams make Rolling Experiment Charts with two columns. Title one column **prediction** and the second column **actual**. 6. Students predict how far they think each ball will roll. Record predictions.	**Create bounce boxes and measure charts** 4. In teams, create bounce boxes and measurement charts (see pictures for ideas). Decorate them with paint and/or markers. Air-dry the paint.
Process: Session 4 30-50 min.	**Classify balls** 6. In teams, closely observe each ball made by team members. Identify attributes of each one. Mark classifications on chart. 7. Count, summarize, and analyze the results.	**Measure rolling distances** 7. Students take turns gently rolling the balls along the measure sheet. Try to use equal force. 8. Measure the distance each ball rolls. Record actual roll distance. 9. Summarize and evaluate the results.	**Predict and measure bounce heights** 5. Position the bounce box on the floor against a wall. Tape the measure chart to a wall next to the bounce box. 6. Create a chart on which to record bounce height predictions and actual results of the experiment. 7. Bounce balls inside the box. Record, compare, and evaluate the results.
		Revise predictions and repeat experiment to verify results.	

Assessment

- Observe students as they classify, measure, and record data. How well do they work together? Are their findings accurately observed, measured, and recorded?
- Ask children to think of and undertake new experiments, such as rolling balls on inclines, counting the number of bounces on different surfaces, and predicting the height a ball will reach rolling down one side of a concave slope and up the other (like a skateboarder's half-pipe). Use measuring skills to record results.
- Ask students to reflect on this lesson and write a DREAM statement to summarize the most important things they learned.

Extensions

For very young students and those with special needs, invite family members to join in the project. Create ball games using measuring skills, such as the Catch-the-Ball Game on Crayola.com. Students play the game and record data on how many times they attempt and succeed at getting the ball in the hole. Hold a tournament and diagram the results of the competition.	Work together using Crayola outdoor products, such as Sidewalk Chalk and Sidewalk Paint. Create courts and play areas on the playground. See directions for Four Squares, Bounce Between Colors on Crayola.com to measure and paint a Four Square court. Play this precision bouncing game as a class. Hold a tournament. Diagram the results of the competition.	Combine results from small groups to form a class graph of results. Use Crayola Sidewalk Chalk and Sidewalk Paint to create a court for the Bottle Tag lesson plan on Crayola.com. Challenge gifted students to experiment more with bouncing balls. Investigate the mathematics of physics by exploring the formulas for determining potential energy and kinetic energy.

Secret Castles: Solve the Number Mysteries!

Objectives

Students identify the elements of architecture through the study of castles and design elements of castle construction.

Students work in small groups using mathematical problem-solving skills to create castles that have numerated features.

Multiple Intelligences

Interpersonal	Spatial
Logical-mathematical	

National Standards

Visual Arts Standard #4 Understands the visual arts in relation to history and cultures	**Mathematics Standards** ***Number and Operations*** Understand numbers, ways of representing numbers, relationships among numbers, and number systems ***Problem Solving*** Apply and adapt a variety of appropriate strategies to solve problems

Background Information

A castle is a large, fortified residence, usually surrounded by thick walls. Traditionally, castles have high windows and towers with numerous features designed to keep the place secure. Size, shape, building materials, and number and orientation of buildings may differ among castles, but they all typically look ornate and stately.

Some walled fortifications date as far back as the walls of Babylon (1600 BCE) and the Qiang Castle in southwest China (111 BCE). The majority of castles in Europe were built during the Middle Ages (1000 to 1500).

The difference between castles and other buildings, such as cathedrals and manors, is that castles served many purposes. Most castles served to defend against invaders, to provide a residence to the powerful lord of the region and his family, and as a symbol of that lord's power over the social structure of the surrounding villages and countryside.

Resources

A Medieval Castle by Fiona MacDonald
Cut-away view of the inside of a medieval castle. Makes learning about castle elements fun. Older students find plenty of richly detailed information in texts and captions.

Castle by David Macauley
Explore the process of constructing a castle, including tools, workers, and materials. Detailed pen and ink illustrations and a compelling storyline. For grades 3 and up.

What Were Castles For? from Usborne Starting Point History
Simple text in a fun presentation of facts about everyday life in a castle. For all ages.

Vocabulary List

Use this list to explore new vocabulary, create idea webs, or brainstorm related subjects.

- Castle functions

Defense	Residence
History	Social structure
Power	Wealth

- Castle features

Arches	Moat
Arrow loops	Towers
Construction materials	Walls
Doors	Windows
Drawbridge	
Flags	

- Examples of castles

Edinburgh
Matsumoto
Neuschwanstein
Palace of Versailles
Prague
Windsor

Artwork created by students from Triangle Elementary School, Hillsborough, New Jersey.
Teacher: Nancy Knutsen

Artwork created by students from
St. Theresa School,
Hellertown, Pennsylvania.

Moats

Windows

Stables

Walls

DOOR

Artwork created by students
from Triangle Elementary School,
Hillsborough, New Jersey.
Teacher: Nancy Knutsen

Secret Castles: Solve the Number Mysteries!

	K-2	3-4	5-6
Suggested Preparation and Discussion	Ask students to describe the buildings they live in. How do you think the builders decided on the number of doors, windows, and floors in the building? Have children count different architectural elements in their homes, school, and other public buildings.		
	Arrange for tables in an open gallery to display finished castles.		
	Create a few Model Magic® castle features for display.		

<table>
<tr><td></td><td>Display photographs and illustrations of castles. Read nonfiction books about castles as well as folk and fairy tales set in castles.

Create an idea web around the concept of castles. Brainstorm what children know about castles, how they are built, and what they look like. Ask children about who lives in a castle and what happens there.

Students form groups of 3 or 4. Explain that each team will work together to build a unique castle.</td><td colspan="2">With students, display books, posters, prints, and other resources about castles. Clearly label photos to identify location and time period, as well as castle elements. Keep a world map nearby to reference. Read historical fiction related to castles and castle-living.

Look at the display of castle photographs. What decisions did castle builders make? What factors influenced their choices? What are some common features in castle construction? What function do you think each feature played in castle life? What 3-D forms can you identify in castle structures?

Students work in small groups to find out how castle features were built, such as…
• shapes, sizes, and mechanics of doors
• height and shape of the keep
• location and design of steps, bridges, and towers
• gate house design and location
Teams brainstorm and sketch features to include in the castles they are going to construct.</td></tr>
</table>

| **Crayola® Supplies** | • Colored Pencils • Glitter Glue • Markers • Model Magic® • Paint • Paint Brushes • School Glue • Scissors • Tempera Mixing Mediums |||

| **Other Materials** | • Craft paper • Index cards • Modeling tools such as plastic dinner knives, craft sticks, and toothpicks • Paper plates • Paper towels • Recycled boxes and cardboard • Recycled cardboard tubes • Recycled newspaper • Ruler • Water containers • White paper |||

| **Set-up/Tips** | • Demonstrate how to cover boxes or other armatures with Model Magic slabs. Show how to press the compound with a craft stick to make it look like stone. Glue any dry pieces together.
• Cover the painting area with newspaper.
• Use paper plates as palettes to combine mixing mediums with tempera paint. Mixing mediums can also be applied before painting and on top of dry paint. |||

Process: Session 1 30-40 min.	**Plan team castles** 1. Ask a volunteer to write numerals 1 through 20 on individual index cards. Turn them over. Each group selects a card in turn until all are taken.	**Plan team castles** 1. On paper, each team writes a list of numerals from 1 to 10.	**Plan team castles** 1. On paper, each team writes a list of numerals from 1 to 20.
	2. Teams use the number cards to plan how many of each feature will be on their castle—doors, windows, flags, towers, and other architectural elements. 3. Teams sketch a plan of what their castle will look like.	2. Ask teams to plan their castles to have one of an architectural feature, two of another feature, three of something else, and so on. The secret to each castle will be to discover how the other teams used number in their designs—so remind teams to keep their lists hidden! 3. Teams work together to sketch their castle plans from different angles (front, back, sides, and from above), paying attention to the 3-D forms that make up the castle structure.	
	4. Teams create lists of steps to construct their castles, materials needed, and who will do what.		

| **Process: Session 2 30-60 min. (may be repeated)** | **Construct castles**
5. Students follow their plans to construct their castles with recycled materials and Model Magic® compound. Suggest that they use their imaginations and problem-solving skills to improve their plans as they work together.
6. Remind teams to measure and use tools to be sure everything on their lists fits together. Prompt students to count each feature to make sure they stick to their plans. Air-dry castles for 24 hours. |||

	K-2	3-4	5-6
Process: Session 3 20-30 min.	**Paint castles** 7. Use Tempera Mixing Mediums to give each castle a unique look. Pearl It! gives the castle a pearly sheen. Glitter It! adds sparkle. Texture It! makes rough, realistic textured walls. Air-dry the paint.		
Process: Session 4 20-30 min.	**Emphasize features** 8. Outline features of castles with markers and glitter glue. Air-dry the glue.	**Add details** 8. Emphasize features on castles with markers and glitter glue. Add more details, such as statues in niches and balustrades. Air-dry.	
Process: Session 5 20-30 min.	**Solve the number mysteries** 9. Students name and label their castles. 10. For each castle, students number a paper from 1 to 10 or 20 as appropriate. Label papers with castle names. Find the secret numbers hidden in each castles' features. Write the feature next to each numeral. 11. Castle builders reveal their secret numbers so students can check their lists.		
Assessment	• Observe students as they brainstorm and collect information about castle features. Note children's use of resources to learn about castle construction and correct castle terminology. • Assess problem-solving skills, teamwork, and use of tools during the planning and construction process. Ask students to explain their team's construction process. • Evaluate student identification and counting of features, both on their own castles and on castles built by other teams. • Ask students to reflect on this lesson and write a DREAM statement to summarize the most important things they learned.		
Extensions	Plan the activity to suit young children and those with disabilities. For example, limit the number of features to 5. Or have two piles of cards, one with numerals and another with features. Children draw a card from each pile to give more structure to the activity. Hold a Builders' Day. Ask parents to donate clean recycled containers and other items. Set up stations around the classroom with different materials to build a variety of different dwellings. Display constructions with child-created labels in a gallery.	Research peasant life. Construct villages outside the castle walls. Challenge students to create their own individual cottages and manors. Check out the Thatched Roof Cottage on Crayola.com for inspiration. Read the *Sir Circumference* books by Cindy Neuschwander. Use each topic to spur an investigation of a math process using the castles. For example, use string to measure the circumference of the castle towers after reading *Sir Circumference and the First Round Table*.	Research castle floor plans. Find out what each room and space was used for. With exceptional students, introduce the concept of scale drawing. To what scale are different floor plans drawn? Each student creates a floor plan for the inside of the team castle. Take into account where doors, windows, and towers are located. Challenge students to measure and use scale.

Castle Along the Rhine
River Germany
Photo by J. McCracken

Ashford Castle
County Mayo, Ireland
Circa 1228 AD
Photo by J. McCracken

Mazes and Labyrinths: Design Your Pathway

Objectives

Students recognize, identify, and navigate through patterns of angles and lines forming the geometric pathways of mazes and labyrinths.

Students (K-2) create simple maze designs on graph paper demonstrating pencil control skills and a basic understanding of lines and right angles.

Students (grades 3-4) use geometric drawing tools and graph paper to demonstrate their understanding of various lines and angles as they create increasingly sophisticated maze or labyrinth designs appropriate to their ages and ability levels.

Student (grades 5-6) research, design, and create a school labyrinth.

Multiple Intelligences

Logical-mathematical

Spatial

What Does It Mean?

Labyrinth: a winding path resembling a spiral, with one entry and one exit, that circles inward to a central point and then out to the exit

Maze: a complex series of paths offering various choices, only one of which eventually leads from one or more starting points to the exit

National Standards

Visual Arts Standard #1	Mathematics Standards
Understands and applies media, techniques, and processes	**Geometry**
	Specify locations and describe spatial relationships using coordinate geometry and other representational systems
	Reasoning and Proof
	Recognize reasoning and proof as fundamental aspects of mathematics

Background Information

Although the terms *maze* and *labyrinth* are often used interchangeably, a labyrinth is actually a winding path that resembles a spiral and circles inward to a central point. There is only one entrance and one exit in a labyrinth. A maze is usually formed by lines and angles. It often has several possible starting points and multiple paths from which to choose, although only one path leads to the exit.

Labyrinths have been found in many ancient cultures and almost always had spiritual significance. In medieval times they were often laid on the floors of cathedrals where they were used as a sort of miniature pilgrimage. Today, some alternative medicine practices use labyrinths as part of the healing environment. Many people fined that labyrinth walking gives them focus, a sense of inner peace, and has spiritual significance.

Mazes, which are a type of puzzle, have offered fascinating challenges to people for centuries. During the Renaissance, gardeners often created 3-D vertical mazes by planting hedges to create complex paths that were difficult to navigate after the shrubs grew above eye level. England's Hampton Court Palace has one such maze for visitors to attempt. Today cornfields are often planted as challenging mazes. Interestingly, corn has been a staple food in Central and South America for centuries, and its name, influenced by Spanish, is maize. Some amusement parks even use mirror mazes to confuse and entertain visitors. 2-D paper mazes are enjoyed in many forms by children as well as adults.

Resources

In Search of Knossos: The Quest for the Minotaur's Labyrinth by Giovanni Caselli
Travel back in time with an archaeologist to explore archaeological digs, architectural finds, and other evidence of the Minoan civilization that lived on Crete. For older elementary students.

King Arthur by Marc Brown
An early elementary read-aloud or middle elementary chapter book. Introduces students to Merlin's maze.

The Amazing Book of Mazes by Adrian Fisher
Extensive history of mazes with many photographs and diagrams to share with children.

Z Goes Home by Jon Agee
Follow the predictable alphabet pattern with unexpected results on every page. Younger children enjoy the story, particular the letter Z's trip into a labyrinth. Older students are intrigued by the use of hard angles and lines in the illustrations.

Vocabulary List

Use this list to explore new vocabulary, create idea webs, or brainstorm related subjects.

- Geometric terms

Acute angle	Parallel
Angle	Pattern
Circle	Pentagon
Curve	Perpendicular
Hexagon	Rectangle
Line	Right angle
Obtuse angle	Square
Octagon	Triangle

- Mazes and labyrinths

Corridor	Mouth
Entrance/Entry	Network
Exit	Passage
Labyrinth	Path
Maze	

Artwork by students from
Mount Prospect Elementary School,
Basking Ridge, New Jersey.
Teacher: Susan Bivona

Mazes and Labyrinths: Design Your Pathway

	K-2	3-4	5-6
Suggested Preparation and Discussion	Display reproductions of labyrinths and mazes. Discuss similarities and differences. Ask students if they have ever walked through a maze or labyrinth. Talk about their feelings in trying to find their way. Provide sample paper mazes for students to trace with their fingers. Use masking tape to outline a maze or labyrinth on the floor for students to walk.		
	Share information about life-size mazes and labyrinths from both ancient and modern times. Share an age-appropriate story about a maze or labyrinth.	Search for specific geometric features in sample mazes and labyrinths: parallel and perpendicular lines; right, acute, and obtuse angles; and geometric shapes formed by the lines, angles, and curves. Ask students to research and share information about the history of mazes and labyrinths. Read the Greek myth of Theseus or some other age-appropriate story.	
	Demonstrate how to draw a geometric maze on graph paper. Include starting and end points as well as some dead ends in the design. Show an example of a template made from glue and how it is used to make crayon rubbings of the maze.		
Crayola® Supplies	• Erasable Colored Pencils		
	• Crayons • Glitter Glue • School Glue		• Sidewalk Chalk
Other Materials	• Graph paper • Straight edges • Triangle templates • White paper		
	• Cardboard • Construction paper • Masking tape		• String • Yardsticks
Set-up/Tips	• Ask K-4 parents and volunteers to collect heavy cardboard for templates. • Practice creating glue designs on recycled paper before beginning a larger, more complex maze. • Place masking tape loops between the rubbing paper and the template to hold them in place for rubbing.		

	K-2	3-4	5-6
Process: Session 1 30-45 min.	**Design simple mazes** 1. On 1-inch graph paper, use a red erasable colored pencil to mark an S (Start) on the left edge and an F (Finish) on the right edge. 2. Draw a simple zigzag path using lines and right angles from S to F, following lines on the graph paper. Erase as needed to adjust the path. This is the "solution" to the maze puzzle. 3. Use contrasting colors to create a tangle of alternate but dead-end paths around the red one. Add rounded as well as zigzag paths. 4. Transfer the maze design to sturdy cardboard. Over-line all maze lines with glue to make a template. Air-dry the glue overnight.	**Design complex mazes** 1. Draw practice mazes using erasable colored pencils on graph paper. Advanced students include more than one start point. Use rulers and triangles to create acute, obtuse, and right angles in the patterns. Include curved paths as well. Erase as needed. Make sure there is a path in and out of the designs! 2. Choose one challenging design to reproduce. 3. Transfer the maze design to sturdy cardboard. 4. Over-line the design with glue to make a template. Air-dry the glue overnight.	**Design a school labyrinth** 1. Research the history and functions of labyrinths. 2. In pairs, create labyrinth sketches on graph paper. 3. Choose a design to reproduce in large scale outdoors. 4. Create a scaled-up plan of the chosen design(s) to reproduce to scale on a playground or another safe location.

Man in the Maze Pendant
Circa 1900s
Artist: Marvin Lucas
2 1/2" x 1/4" with 24" chain
Silver
Private Collection.

	K-2	3-4	5-6

Process: Session 2 30-40 min.

Reproduce and solve mazes

5. Tape plain paper on top of the maze template.

6. Remove a crayon wrapper. Rub the crayon barrel over the paper to reveal a colored print of the maze or labyrinth. Make several copies.

7. Choose a captivating theme for each maze. Embellish the mazes with drawings and words to illustrate the themes.

8. Trade designs with a partner. Trace pathways from start to finish, first with a finger, then with an erasable colored pencil.

9. After the correct path has been identified, overline it with glitter glue. Air-dry.

Create labyrinth

5. Find a safe, large area on a playground to create a labyrinth.

6. Use a yardstick and a ball of string to measure and mark lines from point to point so the lines of the labyrinth correlate to the plan.

Assessment

K-2
- Students review each other's designs to be sure all include one navigable path.
- Do the tracings of graph paper lines show evidence of steady pencil control?
- Ask questions about student designs. What patterns can they identify? What do they notice about the lines and shapes? Do the designs match the chosen themes?

3-4
- Students check that one navigable path exists among several misleading choices. Does the path extend from a starting point on one side of the maze to an exit on the opposite side? How original is the maze theme? Is the maze decorated to reflect the theme?
- Are students able to identify lines, angles, and curves in the designs using correct geometric terms? Do the mazes include several types of angles and/or curved lines?

5-6
- Check that the final labyrinth design is scaled to match the plan.
- How cooperatively did students work with their partners to create the large labyrinth?

- Ask students to reflect on this lesson and write a DREAM statement to summarize the most important things they learned.

Extensions

K-2
Challenge children to work together to create life-size mazes in the classroom using carpet squares laid end to end. Walk the mazes.

Print and share the Johnny Appleseed Maze activity page on Crayola.com.

Incorporate popular story characters into maze designs.

3-4
Set up a Meticulous Mazes learning station with markers and paper. Print directions for Meticulous Mazes from Crayola.com to post at the station. Students create line and angle mazes.

Challenge students to create lift-a-flap mazes with dead-end squares that flip up to display math questions that must be answered correctly to pass.

5-6
Create indoor labyrinths with masking tape.

Turn 2-dimensional line and angle mazes into 3-D designs using Crayola Model Magic compound. Crayola.com shows how to make a Maze in a Box Top.

Work in teams to invent and create labyrinth games. See the Magnetic Mazes lesson plan on Crayola.com.

Challenge advanced students to construct replicas of famous labyrinths.

Children with special needs will benefit from the kinesthetic experience of solving 3-D mazes. If possible, arrange a visit to a local corn or hay bale maze; or with parent volunteers, set up something similar on school grounds.

Encourage inquisitive students to research famous mazes such as the one at England's Hampton Court Palace and report their findings to the class. Older students with an interest in the spiritual or therapeutic significance of labyrinths research and report on those topics.

Covenant Presbyterian Church Labryinth
Napa, California
Photo by R. De Long

Crayola **Dream~Makers**
Building fun and creativity into standards-based learning

The Math of Maps

Objectives

Students (K-2) survey a room, create a map of the room, and then describe the relative spatial relationships of the shapes on the map that represent the objects in the room.

Students (3-4) create a room or school map that visually describes coordinates within the room that specify measured distances between coordinates and indicates directions for moving from one location to another using the map.

Students (5-6) visualize an area in their community from a bird's-eye perspective and compare and contrast the relative proportions of the area.

Students create a two-dimensional treasure hunt map of a three-dimensional area containing distances between one point and another point to find hidden treasures.

Multiple Intelligences

Bodily-kinesthetic
Interpersonal
Logical-mathematical
Naturalist
Spatial

What Does It Mean?

Bird's-eye view: a view from above, as if one were flying over the object

Cartography: the art of creating maps

Scale: accurate proportions when drawing two or more objects

National Standards

Visual Arts Standard #5	Mathematics Standards
Reflects upon and assesses the characteristics and merits of own work and the work of others	**Geometry** Specify locations and describe spatial relationships using coordinate geometry and other representational systems **Measurement** Apply appropriate techniques, tools, and formulas to determine measurements

Background Information

Maps use points, lines, and areas to represent specific spaces. Size, shape, color, orientation, and pattern all help to visually communicate information about a location or how things are distributed over an area. Often points and areas are defined by position with reference to a coordinate system.

Some of the oldest known maps are preserved on Babylonian clay tablets from as far back as 2300 BCE, which is about the same time as the start of Chinese mapmaking. In the first century BCE, the Roman emperor ordered a project to map Roman roads. It took almost 20 years to map 50,000 miles! Pre-Columbian maps in Mexico used footprints to represent roads.

Modern careers in surveying and mapping involve measuring, locating, and establishing lines, angles, elevations, and features—both manufactured and natural—to determine the facts, sizes, and shapes of real locations. Today's cartographers (map-makers) often use multiple computer-driven data sources and design software to create custom maps. Mapmakers also use the math concepts of scale, projection, and a variety of numeric methods to represent locations, including basic coordinate systems.

Resources

Career Ideas for Kids Who Like Math by Diane Lindsey Reeves
Good resource for upper elementary and middle school students interested in math careers. Shows how adults in everyday life apply math.

How Maps Are Made by Martyn Bramwell
Interesting history of early maps. Explains many modern mapmaking techniques. Good introduction to cartography careers for older children.

Mapping Penny's World by Loreen Leedy
Younger students enjoy this story of a little girl who creates maps to help her dog find his hidden toys.

Vocabulary List

Use this list to explore new vocabulary, create idea webs, or brainstorm related subjects.

Areas
Cartographer
Cartography
Color
Coordinate
Distance
Fraction
Key

Large scale
Latitude
Legend
Lines
Longitude
Map
Measurement
Orientation
Pattern

Points
Ratio
Represent
Scale
Shape
Size
Small scale
Symbol
Texture
Value

Artwork by students from Fredon Township School, Newtown, New Jersey.
Teacher: Beth Delaney

Artwork by students from
Fredon Township School,
Newtown, New Jersey.
Teacher: Beth Delaney

	K-2	3-4	5-6

Suggested Preparation and Discussion

Determine safe indoor and/or outdoor environments for this map-making project. Choose a start location for all treasure hunters. Invite adult volunteers to assist children in navigating the environment during data-collection and treasure map assessment.

Ask younger students to describe how to get from the front door of the school to the classroom. What directional words and phrases are helpful? Prompt students to use increasingly precise vocabulary to indicate the directions. If there were a treasure hidden on the school campus, how might a map help them find it?

Display a variety of maps. Include an imaginary pirate's treasure map if possible. Examine the sample maps. What visual elements are effective? How are lines used? What kinds of data are shown? How are specific points marked? How are landmarks indicated? How is distance represented? How do coordinates help indicate locations?

Create a sample map for all students, several treasures, and a decorated box to inspire children's creativity and better understand the construction process.

Demonstrate techniques for shaping air-dry clay by pinching, poking, rolling, or coiling it. Use modeling tools to carve or etch into the clay. Show how to join pieces or smooth edges by dampening the area with a wet finger. Score wide surfaces with a toothpick and press them together.

Set up a table of "treasures" for students to handle. What makes an object a treasure?

The Math of Maps

	K-2	3-4	5-6
Crayola® Supplies	• Air-Dry Clay • Colored Pencils • Crayons • Glitter Glue • Paint Brushes • School Glue • Scissors • Watercolors		
Other Materials	• Measuring tools (U.S. customary and metric) • Modeling tools • Non-standard measuring tools (blocks, boxes, dowel sticks, shoes) • Paper plates • Paper towels • Recycled boxes • Recycled newspapers • Water containers • White paper		
Set-up/Tips	• Paper plates make convenient, portable sculpting surfaces. • Cover the painting area with newspaper. • Ask families to donate clean, recycled boxes.		
Process: Session 1 30-min.	**Survey a space** 1. In pairs, students sketch the space in the classroom. Pay attention to the relative placement of doors, windows, closets, shelves, furniture, and other features. 2. Offer advanced students the option to consider another room for this project.	**Calculate coordinates within a space** 1. Students measure, record, and compare relative lengths of features in the classroom such as the length of the walls, the width of the doors, and the linear length of the windows. 2. Consider other school features such hallways, common spaces, cafeterias, and offices.	**Visualize relative distances between areas** 1. Students identify the relative distance between their homes to another point, such as a friend's home or to a playground. How do the sizes of the land areas compare? 2. Visualize the distance between areas. Consider features that appear between locations such as streets, stores, or community structures.
Process: Session 2 30-45 min. or more	**Sculpt treasures** 3. Students sketch ideas for one or more small, three-dimensional treasures to sculpt from Air-Dry Clay. Urge older students to make intricate, detailed sculptures. Students choose small boxes in which their treasure(s) will fit. 4. Students make the treasures they sketched. Air-dry projects for at least 3 days.		
Process: Session 3 60-90 min.	**Gather map data** 5. Escort students around the area selected for the treasure hunt, perhaps as a school field experience. Ask them to view the area as mapmakers. What are the outer boundaries? How could certain objects in the area be indicated as landmarks on a map? Students secretly choose where they will hide their small boxes containing their treasures.		
	6. Students consider ways to indicate distances between objects and/or boundaries. 7. Talk about ways to measure with a large, actual unit and then how to indicate that distance on a map using a smaller unit. Measure several distances with both standard and nonstandard measuring tools. 8. Note measurements on the map sketches.	6. Students consider how the treasure hunt area looks from above (bird's-eye view). Use metric tools to measure distances between points. 7. Remind students about various approaches to map making. Urge older students to use more sophisticated techniques. They might draw lines from place to place to create an easy map, or plot map points to search for, or make a coordinate grid and provide a series of coordinates for the treasure seeker to follow. 8. Provide metric measuring tools for map making. Students mark the start, finish, and major landmarks. Use tools to measure true distances between points along the path to the treasure. Record measurement data on map sketches.	

General Map of the Discoveries of Admiral de Fonte showing the high possibility of a passage to the Northwest, 1772
Artist: Thomas Jefferys
27 cm x 34 cm
Paris, France
Collection of Barry Goldin.

	K-2	3-4	5-6
Process: Session 4 30-45 min. or more	**Create maps** 9. Use measurement data to create final maps using small items (such as erasers or beads) to indicate nonstandard measurement units. Mark the start, finish, and major landmarks on the maps. 10. Demonstrate how to draw symbols to show the map scale.	**Create maps** 9. Use the map sketches and measurement data to draw treasure maps to scale. 10. Include a compass rose on maps as well as a legend indicating the scale and meaning of symbolic lines, images, and colors.	

Process: Session 5 30 min. or more

Decorate treasures

11. Paint treasures. Use just a little water and add layers of paint for more intense colors. Air-dry the paint.

12. Add sparkle and emphasize details with glitter glue. Air-dry the glue.

Process: Session 6 45 min. or more

Hold a treasure hunt

13. Place finished treasures in boxes, adding packing material to protect them.

14. Create a label to fit on the lid to identify the creator of the treasure. Older students write their names very small and decorate the label. Glue labels on boxes.

15. Take turns secretly hiding the treasures. This may need to be coordinated and done in small groups in confined areas to prevent prematurely finding another child's treasure.

16. Students trade maps to find each other's treasures.

Assessment	• Check that each pair of students completed an accurate survey of a room, created a map of it, and then described the relative spatial relationships of the shapes on the map that represent the objects in the room.	• Check student maps to see that they focus on, and visually describe, coordinates within a room that specify measured distances between coordinates and directions for moving from one location to another using the map.	• Check to see if students visualized and created a map reflective of a community area from a bird's-eye perspective.
		• Check maps for accurate scale and use of lines, points, and coordinate grids to represent the area.	

• Ask students to provide feedback to each other about the accuracy of their maps. Students might offer "two stars and a wish" to each other. Each star is a compliment. The wish is a way to provide constructive feedback: "I wish your map were more clear about…/had more information about…."

• Ask students to reflect on this lesson and write a DREAM statement to summarize the most important things they learned.

Extensions

Young children and those with special needs may benefit from practice with basic directional terms before making their treasure maps. Play a game like Simon Says to move around the room following specific directions using terms such as left, right, 10 steps forward, or west.

Use new mapmaking skills to draw neighborhood maps, local maps, and maps of other pertinent curriculum content.

Use math and mapping words as new vocabulary and spelling words.

Students create coordinate maps of imaginary towns. Include parallel and perpendicular streets as well as buildings in a variety of geometric shapes. Students draw 1-inch square coordinate grids over their maps and prepare a blank coordinate grid. Form partnerships. Without showing their original maps to their partners, students describe their maps using coordinates and correct geometric terms. Partners listen and follow directions to duplicate the imaginary town map on a blank grid. Compare maps. Are they identical? If not, decide what the listener and/or speaker could have done differently.

Encourage students with an interest in research to find out more about the history of mapmaking including challenges faced by early cartographers from various civilizations. How did early Egyptians make their own paper? See Egyptian Papyrus Paper on Crayola.com for directions and make your own paper for a new treasure map.

Explore the math of projection mapping. How do cartographers create flat maps of a round planet?

Estimate a Pot's Capacity

Objectives

Students create decorative pots reflective of various cultures.

Students explore how the same amount of modeling compound (measured by volume) can be used to create pots with different capacities.

Students (K-2) identify each pot's capacity and then order their pots according to capacity.

Students (grades 3-4) select and apply appropriate standard units of measure to determine the capacity of their pots.

Students (grades 5-6) select and apply the conversion of appropriate customary systems of measure to metric units of measure to determine the capacity of their pots.

Multiple Intelligences

Logical-mathematical
Spatial

National Standards

Visual Arts Standard #2 Using knowledge of structures and functions **Visual Arts Standard #4** Understands the visual arts in relation to history and culture	**Mathematics Standards** ***Measurement*** Understand measurable attributes of objects and the units, systems, and processes of measurement ***Connection*** Recognize and apply mathematics in contexts outside of mathematics

Background Information

Clay has been used by many cultures throughout history to create dishware, cooking pots, storage utensils, vases, and other objects. Because clay is inexpensive and easy to find, many of these objects were used and thrown away, but some very old examples have survived. Their form and design make it possible to conclude something about their function as well as the culture that produced them. Often these vessels held liquids such as oil or water. Others were used to store grain for the next planting season. Some pots were very large while others were very small.

Artists often use unique shapes and surface designs that make it possible to recognize the cultural origins. Decorations and patterns carved or painted onto ancient clay vessels often depict the folk stories, history, or beliefs of the culture. Figures from mythology appear on many ancient Greek vases, while many Native American tribes decorated their vessels with distinctive geometric designs.

Resources

A Single Shard by Linda Sue Park
Set in a 12th-century Korean village known for its pottery. Novel invites readers to join a 13-year-old as he learns the potter's craft from a master. Newbury Award winner inspires discussion.

Ceramics by Ruth Kassinger
Science and history of pottery as well as the cultural myths associated with many works. Intrigues older readers. Colorful illustrations inspire all ages.

The Pot That Juan Built by Nancy Andrews-Goebel
Playful, rhyming, informative text. Introduces readers to Juan Quezada, a noted Mexican potter. Information about both the art and science of pottery appeals to a wide audience. Bright, colorful illustrations.

Vocabulary List

Use this list to explore new vocabulary, create idea webs, or brainstorm related subjects.

- Pottery process

Clay	Seal
Coil	Shape
Firing	Slab
Glaze	Slip
Join	Vessel
Kiln	Wheel
Pinch	

- Exterior decoration

Burnishing	Punctuation
Embossing	Stamping
Incision	

- Archaeology of pottery

Date	Technological
Form	innovation
Function	Themes
Level of	Trade pattern
stratification	

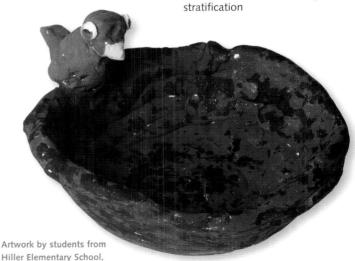

Artwork by students from
Hiller Elementary School,
Madison Heights, Michigan.
Teacher: Craig Hinshaw

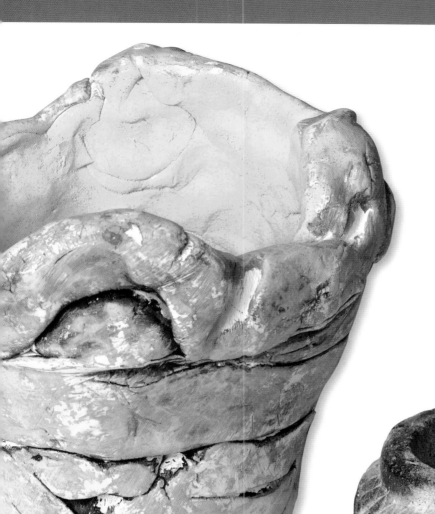

What Does It Mean?

Capacity: the amount of liquid or other measurable material a vessel can hold

Coil: sculpting technique using long coils ("snakes") of compound. Coils are wrapped around an armature or held in place to form an empty vessel

Pinch: technique to sculpt a pot from a lump of compound by pressing into the middle with the thumbs and rotating to hollow out the interior

Slab technique: modeling compound is rolled or pressed flat, then cut into shapes and sealed together to form the bottom and sides of a vessel. Edges are smoothed to complete the sculpture

Volume: measure, in cubic units, of the amount of space a 3-D object occupies

American Indian Vessel
Mound builder culture
Artist unknown
Carved Stone
4" x 5"
Collection of Kevin Zelienka.

Artwork by students from
Hiller Elementary School,
Madison Heights, Michigan.
Teacher: Craig Hinshaw

Acoma Polychrome Pottery
Artist: Lucy Lewis
Clay and paint
6" x 4 1/2"
Private Collection.

Santa Clara, San Ildefonso Pot
Artist unknown
Carved, burnished clay
6" x 3 1/2"
Private Collection.

Crayola **Dream~Makers®**
Building fun and creativity into standards-based learning

Estimate a Pot's Capacity

	K-2	3-4	5-6
Suggested Preparation and Discussion	Display examples of pottery in a variety of styles from different eras and cultures. Invite children to describe what they see. Draw conclusions about how the pottery may have been used and who created it. Through creation of their own pottery, students will demonstrate an understanding of how form and function are interrelated and the role culture plays in the decorative arts.		
	Ask children questions such as: How do people use ceramics today? What are some of the items you use that are made from clay? Show how to estimate and measure the liquid capacity of different vessels. Experiment with nonstandard measures such as marbles or aquarium gravel.	Review the concept of capacity by experimenting with how different sized containers hold varying amounts of water and nonstandard units of measure such as marbles. Explore how two vessels with different shapes may hold equal amounts of water. Show how one vessel may have a capacity equal to two other vessels (i.e., 2 cups equals 1 pint).	Consider how pottery has changed over the ages. Examine several ceramic styles. Discuss what each can reveal about the society and time period from which it comes. Research the history of pottery, including the science of clay and ceramics. Research and identify the differences between the U.S. customary system of measure and the metric system of measure.
	Measure the volume of blocks and boxes of different sizes using measuring tools, units, and calculators if necessary to compute length x width x height. Younger students might measure cubic inch cubes and then build structures with them, counting the cubes to measure the volume of the structures. Discuss and demonstrate basic modeling techniques such as how to pinch clay into shapes to make pinch pots, how to roll it to create coils and slabs, and how to join pieces by adding a bit of water and scoring with a tool. Demonstrate pottery-decorating techniques using tools to create indentations, imprints, and lines on the pot's surface.		
Crayola® Supplies	• Air-Dry Clay or Model Magic® • Markers • Paint Brushes • Tempera Mixing Mediums: Pearl It!, Glitter It!, Texture It! • Watercolors		
Other Materials	• Chart paper • Modeling tools (plastic dinner knives, craft sticks, toothpicks) • Paper plates • Recycled newspaper • Water containers		
	• Marbles	• Aquarium gravel • Measuring cups	
Set-up/Tips	• Cover work surface with recycled newspaper. Sculpt, air-dry, and paint modeling compound on paper plates. • Add drops of water to Air-Dry Clay if it starts to dry while sculpting. • Air-dry the pottery completely before experimenting with capacity. • Glaze painted pottery with a glaze of equal parts of school glue and water or with mixing mediums for added surface strength. • Pots are for decorative use only. They are not intended to hold or store liquids.		
Process: Session 1 30-45 min.	## Sculpt and embellish pots 1. Form a tennis-ball size lump of either Air-Dry Clay or Model Magic compound into cubes. Measure cubes (length x width x height). Adjust cube sizes so all are approximately the same volume of modeling compound. 2. Form vessels with the compound. Use pinch, coil, and/or slab techniques to build the pottery form. What variations in pot structures might affect capacities? 3. With modeling tools, decorate the surface. Children's decorative styles should be increasingly elaborate as their skills mature. Air-dry Model Magic for 24 hours. Air-dry clay pots for 3 days.		
Process: Session 2 30-45 min.	## Decorate pots 4. Decorate the surface of the pot with watercolors. Older children's decorations should be more detailed and sophisticated. Air-dry the paint.		
Process: Session 3 20 min.	## Add finishing touches 5. Paint at least one coat of a Crayola Mixing Medium or a glaze of glue on the pot if desired. Air-dry the coating.		

	K-2	3-4	5-6
Process: Session 4 30-45 min.	**Determine pot capacity**	**Measure pot capacity**	**Measure and convert pot capacity**
	6. Explain that marbles will be used as units of capacity. Students estimate how many marbles it will take to fill their pots. Record estimates on a chart.	6. Create a chart with two columns: U.S. Customary Estimate, and U.S. Customary.	6. Create a chart with four columns: U.S. Customary Estimate, U.S. customary, Metric Estimate, and Metric.
	7. Students fill their pots to the rim with marbles, counting as they do so. Record how many marbles each pot holds on the chart.	7. Estimate the capacity of pots in U.S. customary (fluid ounces) units. Record estimates on the chart.	7. Students estimate the capacity of their pots in both metric (milliliter) and U.S. customary (fluid ounces) units. Record estimates on the chart.
	8. Arrange pots in order from highest capacity to lowest capacity. What are the factors that determine how much a vessel will hold? Does the shape of the pot matter? What about the thickness of the pot walls?	8. Fill pots with aquarium gravel. Empty gravel into measuring cups to determine the approximate capacity of each vessel. Record U.S. customary measures on the chart.	8. Students fill their pots with aquarium gravel. Empty the gravel into measuring cups to determine the approximate capacity of each vessel. Record research findings on the chart.
Assessment	• Each child uses the demonstrated hand-building techniques to create a vessel.	• Students successfully use basic hand-building techniques to create pottery.	• Students successfully create a pot using one of the three hand-building pottery techniques.
	• Students estimate the capacity of their vessels using marbles as units of measure.	• Students check the accuracy of U.S. customary measures for one another's pots.	• Students check one another's measurements and conversions for accuracy.
	• Children measure actual capacity using marbles, counting correctly.		

• Students correctly record and thoughtfully analyze their research findings. Students draw conclusions about how the structures of pots affect their capacity.

• Ask students to reflect on this lesson and write a DREAM statement to summarize the most important things they learned.

Extensions	Try Pinch a Pot of Petals on Crayola.com to make pinch pots. Estimate and measure capacities of these new vessels.	Explore the treasure of Chinese porcelain, using the Pretend Porcelain lesson plan on Crayola.com.	Advanced students research pottery from various cultures and present their findings to the class.
	Ask parents to donate a variety of clean, recycled containers for students to use to practice their estimation and measuring skills. Use different materials to measure capacity of containers. Provide measuring cups.	Create Measure Up! Capacity Charts to visualize how the units measure up. See this Lesson Plan on Crayola.com. Ask parents to donate safe, clean, recycled, cylindrical containers, such as snack and film canisters. Children fill cylinders with water to measure the capacity of those of different widths and heights.	Classmates form small groups representing different cultures to create replicas of their pottery for display. Include colorful maps and information boards.

   Explore the concept of volume and capacity with younger students and those with special needs by conducting the following experiment: Students drop golf balls or other similar items, one at a time, into an unbreakable container half filled with water. What happens? What conclusions can they draw? Can students suggest a way of measuring exactly 1 cup of peanut butter, margarine, or a similar product making use of the water-displacement theory demonstrated?

   Mathematically talented students research the work of Archimedes, especially his water-displacement theory. Share findings with the class including the story of his bathtub discovery. Is this story fact or fiction?

What Are the Chances?

Objectives

Students predict the probability of how many times a particular number will appear in a random sequence and record the results.

Grade 3-6 students observe how artists from the Pop-Art movement used line and color to define space.

Students initiate a grid of random shapes, randomly select colors to fill the shapes, and count the results.

Students compare their predictions with their results.

Grade 3-6 students express their data in mathematical terms and graph the results.

Multiple Intelligences

Logical-mathematical

Spatial

What Does It Mean?

Benday screening: silkscreen printing process using a pattern of dots to create images

Pop Art: art movement of the 1950s and 60s in which artists were inspired by images from mass media

National Standards

Visual Arts Standard #3 Chooses and evaluates a range of subject matter, symbols, and ideas	**Mathematics Standards** *Data Analysis and Probability* Understand and apply basic concepts of probability *Grades 5-6* *Representation* Create and use representations to organize, record, and communicate mathematical ideas

Background Information

Want to win a lottery? Or predict the weather? The study of probability helps people figure out the likelihood of something happening. If you are using a spinner or rolling a number cube, you might want to know how likely you are to get a certain number.

If there are five different numbers on a spinner (1, 2, 3, 4, 5), you have a one in five chance of spinning any one of the numbers. The probability (or chance) of spinning any one of these 5 numbers can be expressed by a fraction (1/5) or a decimal (0.20), in a range from 0 to 1. Events that are very likely to happen would have a probability near 1, such as spinning a number (the pointer might land on a dividing line). Events that are unlikely to happen would have a probability near 0, such as the spinner stopping on a line. Probability can also be expressed by a percentage (such as a 20% chance of spinning a 4 when there are 5 numbers on the spinner).

When figuring out the probability of an event happening, it is important to first identify all of the outcomes that could possibly occur (the sample space). For example, when predicting the weather, consider the possibility of all different kinds of weather first. Then look at other factors to determine the likelihood of each type of weather event. When considering the probability of a weather event for a particular day, the National Weather Service looks at all other days in their historical database that have the same weather characteristics (such as temperature, pressure, humidity) and may determine, for example, that on 70% of similar days in the past, it rained.

Resources

Getting to Know the World's Greatest Artists: Roy Lichtenstein by Mike Venezia
Introduces students to Roy Lichtenstein's Pop Art and his use of flat colors and trademark Benday dots. Bright reproductions and easily understood text will inspire students of all ages.

Probably Pistachio by Stuart J. Murphy
Playful introduction to probability for all ages. Older students may enjoy calculating the probability of events in the book happening to them!

Uncle Andy's by Jamie Warhol
A warm, personal, child's eye view of Pop artist Andy Warhol on a visit to his New York City apartment. Children in grades 1-4 will learn about the creative process as they observe Warhol through the eyes of his young nephew.

Vocabulary List

Use this list to explore new vocabulary, create idea webs, or brainstorm related subjects.

- Mathematical terms

Certain	Likely	Outcome
Chance	Lines	Predict
Decimal	Diagonal	Percentage
Even chance	Intersecting	Probability
Event	Parallel	Random
Fraction	Perpendicular	Sequence
Graph	Occurrence	Sample space
Impossible	Odds	Unlikely

- Art terms
Benday screening
Cartoon
Color
Comic strip
Pattern
Pop Art
Popular culture
Primary colors
Space

Random number generators and container
Artist unknown
Private Collection.

Artwork by students from
Oakhurst Elementary School
Fort Worth, Texas.
Teacher: Amanda Warner Grantz

Artwork by students from
St. Theresa School,
Hellertown, Pennsylvania.

	K-2	3-4	5-6

Suggested Preparation and Discussion

Introduce the concept of probability by creating a spinner with numerals 1, 2, and 3 on it. Each child divides paper or a white board into three columns and writes a 1, 2, or 3 at the top of each column. Children take turns spinning. All children tally how many times each number is spun. Add the tally marks for each number. Talk about the results. Discuss the meaning of the word *random*. Explain that the chance of a number being spun is called the *probability*.

Read *Probably Pistachio* to the class.

Brainstorm familiar games that involve probability (such as BINGO).

Review the concept of probability. Students brainstorm examples of where probability is used in daily life (weather predictions, lottery results, batting averages).

Look at work by Roy Lichtenstein, Piet Mondrian, and/or Joan Miro. Note how their compositions fill the space on a page. Show students how these artists use lines and color to define space.

With students, develop and post a list of ways surface space can be divided using mathematical terms such as intersecting lines, circles, and triangles.

What Are the Chances?

	K-2	3-4	5-6
Crayola® Supplies	• Colored Pencils • Crayons • Markers		
Other Materials	• Drawing paper • Random number selectors (such as number cubes or spinners) • Rulers • White paper		
	• Colored counters (optional)		

	K-2	3-4
Process: Session 1 15-20 min.	**Create color grids** 1. In small groups, students take turns folding drawing paper until it has several crisscrossing lines. Unfold the paper. 2. Children trace over fold lines with a black marker to make a grid-like design of random shapes. 3. Teams count the number of spaces in their designs. Suggest that students lightly mark each space as it is counted or place a colored counter in the space as they count it.	**Create grids** 1. In small groups, students work together to create a grid by filling drawing paper with lines and shapes using colored pencils. Make sure sections are neither extremely large nor extremely small. 2. Trace lines with a black marker. 3. Count the number of spaces.
Process: Session 2 20-30 min.	**Predict and choose color codes** 4. To determine how to color each space of the design, students choose colors at random using a number cube and a color code. On a chart (see sample), teams choose a color code to match every possible outcome on the number cube (such as 1 = red, 2 = yellow). 5. Teams predict how many times they think each number will be rolled, taking into account the total number of spaces on the grids. 6. Children arrange colored counters to show their predictions for each number and after they have reached agreement, they record these predictions on the chart.	**Predict probabilities** 4. To determine how to color each space of the design, students choose colors at random using a number generator (such as a number cube or spinner) and a color code. Each group chooses and/or creates a random number generator and then compiles a chart that lists the possible numbers that could be selected (see sample). Teams create their own color codes for every possible outcome (such as 1 = red, 2 = yellow). 5. Teams work together to predict and record on the chart how often each number will be generated, given the total number of spaces on the grid. 6. Students evaluate their predictions to discuss the probability of each number/color being rolled. Use terms with a range such as *impossible – unlikely – even chance – likely – certain* to express the probability of each prediction.

7. Students take turns generating random numbers. Write each number generated in a separate space in the color grid until all spaces are filled.

8. When all sections are numbered, students count how many times each number was randomly chosen. How do the actual results compare with the team's original predictions?

Process: Session 3 20-30 min.	**Add colors and patterns** 9. Color each space of the design according to their selected color codes. Use solid colors or patterns, but only one color in each space. Show work by Roy Lichtenstein as an example.

	K-2	3-4	5-6
Process: Session 4 15-20 min.	**Reflect on results** 10. Talk about the results of randomly generating numbers and associated colors. Were any colors used more than the others? Did any colors appear significantly fewer times? Compare results among teams.	**Express probabilities and graph results** 10. Students calculate the probability of each number being generated based on the actual data.	
		11. Students express results as fractions, with the numerator indicating how many times each number was rolled and the denominator indicating how many total rolls were made. 12. Students graph the results of their experiments using the data in the chart.	11. Students express the actual results as decimals and percentages. Compare actual results to predictions. Draw conclusions. 12. Use the information on the chart to graph the data using a computer.
Assessment	• Observe children at each step of the process, asking questions to assess understanding of probability.	• Compare predictions, calculations, graphs, and artwork. Discuss observations. Use appropriate math vocabulary to describe designs.	
	• Review records of predictions and results for accuracy. • Ask students to reflect on this lesson and write a DREAM statement to summarize the most important things they learned.		
Extensions	For younger students, first create colorful spinners to explore the probability of an event occurring when there are 2, 3, 4, and 5 possible outcomes. Show students how to record the results in columns on the graph paper and then tally the results. Students with special needs may find it less confusing to use random color selectors (a spinner with colors) rather than random number selectors.	Challenge students to create their own probability games with Heads 'n Tails™ Colored Pencils. See Flip Coins for Fun: A Tossing Game on Crayola.com. Create individual Pop Art drawings in the styles of Lichtenstein and Warhol. Fill spaces with colors determined by chance.	Generate a list of questions, predict the probability of different answers, and then poll a group. See Slanted Surveys and Statistics on Crayola.com for a lesson plan to explore how statistics can be misleading. Encourage students with a strong interest in art history or research to study the works of artists associated with Pop Art. Share findings with the class. Discuss messages they feel the artists were trying to convey.

Sample Chart Using a Six-Sided Random Number Generator

Number of spaces on the grid: _____

Number	Color choice for the number	Predictions (How many times will the number be rolled?)	Probability (Grades 3-6) *impossible – unlikely – even chance – likely – certain*	Results (How many times WAS the number rolled?)	Actual probability (expressed as a fraction— grades 3-4; in decimals and percentages— grades 5-6)
1					
2					
3					
4					
5					
6					

Symmetrical Starburst

Objectives

Students (K-2) recognize, name, and draw kite shapes, examples of radial symmetry, and assess how various viewers' responses differ to the work.

Students (grades 3-4) investigate, describe, and reason about the results of subdividing, combining, and transforming shapes.

Students (grades 5-6) examine the congruence, similarity, and line or rotational symmetry of a paper object using transformations.

Students describe their radial designs using geometry vocabulary that address grade-level standards.

Multiple Intelligences

- Interpersonal
- Linguistic
- Logical-mathematical
- Naturalist
- Spatial

What Does It Mean?

Congruent: shapes coincide exactly when superimposed

Kite folds: paper-folding method that results in a sled-kite shape (see diagram)

Radial symmetry: when objects or sections fan out in a regular pattern from a central point

National Standards

Visual Arts Standard #5 Reflects upon and assesses the characteristics and merits of own work and the work of others	**Mathematics Standards** *Communication* Communicate their mathematical thinking coherently and clearly to peers, teachers, and others *Geometry* Apply transformations and use symmetry to analyze mathematical solutions Use visualization, spatial reasoning, and geometric modeling to solve problems

Background Information

Radial symmetry is evident when regularly arranged objects or sections radiate from a central point or axis. Examples of radial symmetry can be found in both nature and in human-made objects. Spider webs and cacti often display radial symmetry. In the sea, five-rayed radial body symmetry is characteristic of echinoderms such as feather stars, sea stars, and sea urchins.

Radial symmetry is a feature seen in some works of Op Art, in rosette windows, and also in a relatively new craft form, tea bag folding. Begun several years ago in Holland, this new art form developed by chance as a Dutch woman named Tiny van der Plas as she was sipping tea. She folded and arranged the decorative envelopes that come wrapped around European tea bags. Using some basic techniques similar to Japanese origami, this art also involves careful arrangement of folded paper in a kaleidoscope fashion, demonstrating radial symmetry.

Resources

Starfish, Urchins, and Other Echinoderms by Daniel Gilpin
Colorful photos of radial symmetry in nature. Sure to inspire all ages.

Teatime With Emma Buttersnap by Lindsey Tate
Discover the origins of tea, teatime, and customs surrounding the consumption of the beverage. Introduces the art of tea-bag folding.

Vocabulary List

Use this list to explore new vocabulary, create idea webs, or brainstorm related subjects.

Angles	Congruence	Radial
Acute angle	Fraction	Reflective
Obtuse angle	Line	Rotation
Right angle	Midpoint	Shape
Axis	Mirror-image	Similar
Balance	Motif	Symmetry
Circular	Op-Art	
Color	Pattern	

Mola radial design
Artist unknown
12" x 10"
Cotton, cotton thread
Private Collection.

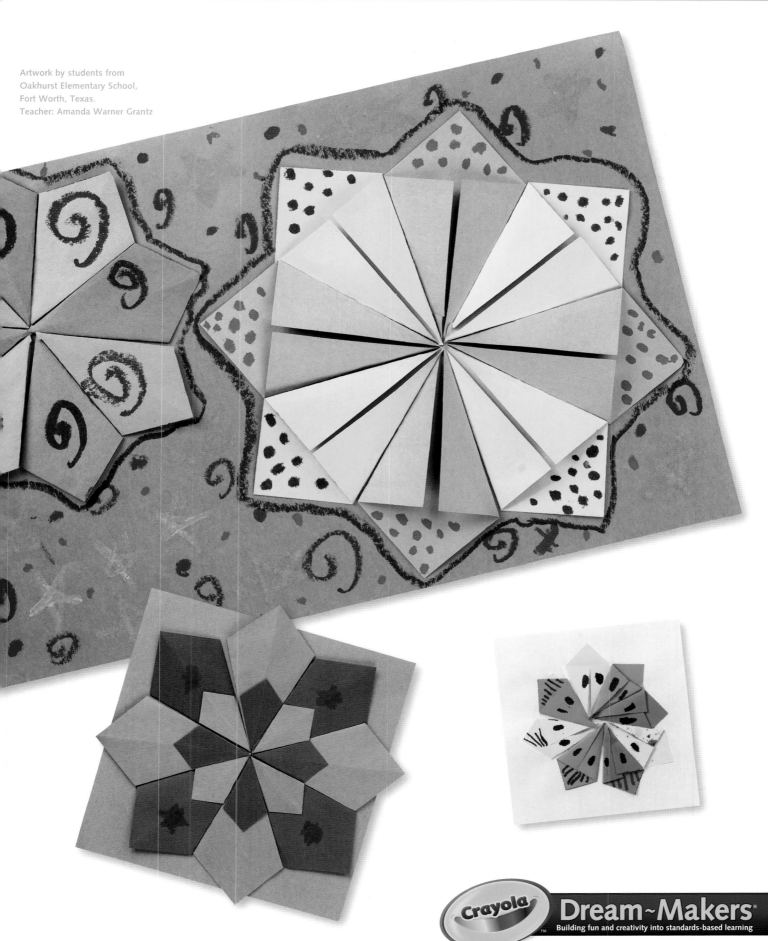

Artwork by students from
Oakhurst Elementary School,
Fort Worth, Texas.
Teacher: Amanda Warner Grantz

Symmetrical Starburst

	K-2	3-4	5-6
Suggested Preparation and Discussion	Display books, photographs, and art samples of radial symmetry. Include photographs of spider webs and sea animals, abstract art from artists like M.C. Escher, and examples of tea-bag folding. In a circle of students, pass around one display item. Ask each child to look at it and think of one word that comes to mind. Ask students to share their words. Talk about how different students saw different things in the item. Repeat activity with other items. Create examples of folded-paper shapes and final artwork. Demonstrate paper folding and other steps as needed.		
			Look at a folded-paper kite. Students describe the geometry of the kite as viewed from the folded side and unfolded side. Identify shapes and angles.
Crayola® Supplies	• Colored Pencils • Glue • Markers • Scissors • Slick Stix™ Crayons		
Other Materials	• Construction paper • Rulers		
Process: Session 1 30-45 min. or more	**Fold kite shapes** 1. Children each measure and cut drawing paper into a 12-inch square. Encourage students to help each other. 2. Hold the paper square in a diamond formation with corners pointing up, down, and to the sides. See the diagram for folding directions. 3. Figure out how many kite sections are needed to create a circular radial design. 4. Cut that many more squares and fold them.	**Fold kite shapes** 1. Measure and cut colored paper into 2-, 3-, and 4-inch squares. Make eight squares in each size. Kite-fold all squares. Encourage students to help each other. 2. Cut a 12-inch square of colored paper. Use a ruler to find and mark the midpoint. 3. Hold a small paper square in a diamond formation with corners pointing up, down, and to the sides. See the diagram for folding directions. 4. Repeat folds with all small squares so that the subdivision and combining of sections will transform the shapes and create a starburst design.	
Process Session 2 30-45 min. or more	**Form the radial design** 5. Assemble kites into a simple circular, radial design. 6. Glue them to construction paper. Air-dry the glue. 7. Color the faces of both the folded sections and the inside of the folds. Make sure that the drawings reflect symmetry in color, shape, and pattern.	**Transform shapes into a symmetrical design** 5. Experiment with symmetrical patterns. One way is to arrange the one size of kite around the midpoint. Repeat the experiment with the other two sizes. 6. Choose which size to arrange first. Glue kites around the midpoint in a symmetrical pattern. 7. Tuck another size of kites into the attached kites to form a second layer. Glue them in place on construction paper. Repeat with the remaining kites. Air-dry glue.	**Create symmetrical congruent shapes** 5. Experiment with different ways folded papers can be arranged around the midpoint to make a balanced radial design, such as: • Side-by-side, fold down • Side-by-side, fold up • Smaller kites arranged with tips nested in larger kites, fold down or up • Folded arms of different colors and sizes linked 6. Think of unique arrangements. Share ideas for other arrangements that show balanced radial symmetry using only the kites made. 7. Glue final designs on construction paper so they are congruent. Air-dry glue.

Berks County Barn Hex Sign
Photo by R. De Long

	K-2	3-4	5-6

Process:
Session 3
15-20 min.

Embellish designs

8. Embellish symmetrical shapes with patterns that support the radial symmetry of the design, such as: outline shapes in a similar way around the design; add dots, dashes, or lines of colors similar to kites; and add shapes around the design on the background paper.

Assessment

- Observe students for accuracy and ability to follow directions as they measure papers, fold kites, measure to find the midpoint, and experiment with radial designs.

• Students assemble kite shapes into a circular symmetrical design.	• Students exchange work and check each other's art for results that illustrate an understanding of accurate subdivision and combing of shapes that transforms sections into a symmetrical, radial design.	• Examine art for congruent sections that are similar and are transformed into a starburst.

- Display finished art. Students observe and reflect on what they see. Discuss impressions, comparisons, unique arrangements, embellishment ideas, and use of colors. Identify elements that contribute to radial symmetry. Locate and identify different kinds of angles and shapes in the designs.

- Ask students to reflect on this lesson and write a DREAM statement to summarize the most important things they learned.

Extensions

Experiment with arranging and layering tangram shapes around a central point. Make paper kites to decorate the classroom. See Easy Breezy Kite on Crayola.com for decorating ideas. Set up a kite-folding activity center. Show children how to fold kites in half for another shape option. Fold, arrange, and decorate radial designs with any number of kites.	Be geometry detectives! Use paper-folding skills to create another 3-dimensional work of art with lots of angles to measure and identify. See the Tin Foil Twinkles lesson plan on Crayola.com for complete directions. The craft of tea-bag folding has grown beyond tea bag envelopes. Crafters often create decorative papers to fold and arrange. Lead children to design their own deco-rative paper with radial symmetry, using only a black outline of the design. Copy designs to color. Use designed paper to create kites to arrange in new radial designs.	Gather decorative papers. Cut them into different-size squares. Create half kites (kite folded in half, joining side tips) and pentagon kites (lower corner folded up to meet upper corner). Challenge students to create unique radial designs. Measure the lines and angles of the radial designs. Repeat the shapes, lines, and angles with 2-dimensional art materials on paper. Explore more color, line, space, and angles with the Shapes and Angles lesson plan on Crayola.com.

Make detailed colored pencil drawings of symmetry in nature, such as spider webs, flowers, or cacti.

How to make kite folds

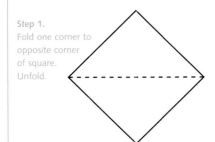

Step 1.
Fold one corner to opposite corner of square. Unfold.

Step 2.
Bring bottom left edge up to meet the crease.

Step 3.
Bring top left edge down to meet the crease.

Stock-Smart Art

Objectives

Students increase their vocabulary and understanding of basic business investment terminology.

Students examine sample stock certificates and then create imaginary certificate designs for modern businesses.

Students in grades K-2 use the value of various coins to calculate imaginary stock values and write algebraic equations using those values.

Students in grades 3-6 identify how investments benefit individual investors as well as businesses.

Multiple Intelligences

Interpersonal
Logical-mathematical
Spatial

What Does It Mean?

Scripophily: the hobby of collecting stock and bond certificates for their artistic and historic value rather than their financial value

National Standards

Visual Arts Standard #4 Understanding the visual arts in relation to history and culture	**Mathematics Standards** ***Number and Operations*** Compute fluently and make reasonable estimates ***Problem-Solving*** Solve problems that arise in mathematics and other contexts ***Representation*** Create and use representations to organize, record, and communicate mathematical ideas

Background Information

Business organizations that are formed to manufacture goods, develop new technology, or deliver products and services are most commonly formed as **corporations**. Often, groups of people share in the ownership of a corporation. Each unit of ownership is called a **share**. Shares (also called **stocks**) can be purchased by individuals or groups. A corporation uses money from investors to build its business. A stock certificate is a paper document reflecting legal ownership of a specific number of shares in a corporation.

Stock certificates are one way to grasp a visual picture of the historic development of industrial growth in the United States. These documents meld art and economics. For example, 19th-century railroad corporations stamped locomotives on their certificates, and early automobile companies incorporated popular Art Deco motifs. Today's media giants use sleek, modern graphics.

Vintage certificates included lively text offering historic background on companies. Many older certificates printed in several colors and featuring fine embellished engravings are treated as rare, numbered, limited edition prints. These historic certificates are often framed and hung on office walls.

The act of collecting stock certificates is known as *scripophily*. Particularly valuable to collectors are those signed by the historically important industrialists who owned the companies, such as John D. Rockefeller, who started the Standard Oil Company of Ohio in 1862. A very rare stock certificate from the late 18th-century Philadelphia and Lancaster Turnpike is printed on sheepskin.

Today, paper stock certificates are becoming rare and often people who want them must pay more.

Resources

Alexander, Who Used to Be Rich Last Sunday by Judith Viorst
Connects younger students' experiences with money. Alexander is a familiar character in children's literature.

Money Sense for Kids by Hollis Page Harman
Older students learn about saving, spending, and investing money. Comprehensive, yet enjoyable, book about the basics of economics.

The Art of the Market: Two Centuries of American Business as Seen Through Its Stock Certificates by Bob Tamarkin
A look at stock certificates and their value in the worlds of both art and American economic history. Students of all ages enjoy decorative elements in the certificates illustrated.

Ups And Downs: A Book About the Stock Market by Nancy Lowwen and Brian Jensen
An introduction to corporations, shares, stocks, and how investment can benefit both businesses and individuals.

Vocabulary List

Use this list to explore new vocabulary, create idea webs, or brainstorm related subjects.

- Business terms

Asset	Money
Business	Ownership
Buy	Payout
Cash	Profit
Claim	Reinvest
Corporation	Save
Dividend	Sell
Earnings	Share
Gain	Shareholder
Growth	Spend
Investment	Stock
Loss	Stock certificate
Market	

- Art terms

Art Deco	Pattern
Border	Style
Design	Texture
Embellish	Vintage
Graphics	Visual
Image	

Artwork created by students and teacher from Princeton North Elementary School, Princeton, Minnesota. Teacher: Tom Tschumper

	K-2	3-4	5-6
Suggested Preparation and Discussion	Review concepts of money. Display real bills and coins to identify. Talk about their design. Ask children how people earn, spend, and save money. Talk about banks and their role in helping people manage their money. Ask children to name some familiar toy companies, stores, or restaurants. Explain that one way people make money is by buying a **share** of a company. When the company makes money it shares that money, called **profits**, with **shareholders**. Often when people buy shares (or **stock**), they get a special paper from the company called a **stock certificate**.	Review concepts of money and investments. Some people collect old stock certificates as a hobby. This is called *scripophily*. Ask students to display copies of stock market reports from newspapers or Web sites. As a class, select several stocks. Track them over a period of time and chart the rise and/or fall of their values. Calculate percentage of change in value. Students in grades 5 and 6 also determine median, mode, and range. Discuss how changes in the stock market affect individual investors and companies. Invite families who own stock to visit the classroom to show their certificates and talk about stocks they own. Consider inviting an investment broker to speak with the class.	

Show examples of actual or reproduction stock certificates. Encourage students to examine borders, logos, illustrations, signatures, and texts.

Redesign a familiar, publicly held company's stock certificate and show the new version to students to inspire their creativity.

Crayola **Dream~Makers**®
Building fun and creativity into standards-based learning

Stock-Smart Art

	K-2	3-4	5-6
Crayola® Supplies	• Crayons	• Colored Pencils	
	• Glitter Glue • Watercolor Paint • Paint Brushes		
Other Materials	• Coins		
	• Paper towels • Recycled newspaper • Water containers • White paper		
Set-up/Tips	• Cover art surface with recycled newspaper.		
	• Demonstrate how to make crayon rubbings and do watercolor resist.		
	• Students can hold papers for each other while they do rubbings. Or tape coins to a table surface to hold them in place before rubbing. Sharper images will result.		

Process: Session 1 30-45 min.

Design a make-believe stock certificate

1. Students each select a favorite company for which to design a new stock certificate.
2. Make border designs by placing coins under paper and rubbing over them with crayons.
3. Embellish the certificates with colorful words, lines, shapes, and patterns.

Redesign stock certificates

1. Select a publicly held company. Research its history and products.
2. Using this information, use crayon to design a new certificate for the company's stockholders.
3. Include a company name, decorative border, a sign or symbol in a style that reflects the company's product, space for signatures of company leaders, and other decorative features. Consider line, shape, color, texture, and pattern in the design.

4. With watercolors, emphasize specific parts of the stock certificate designs. Air-dry the paint.

Process: Session 2 30-45 min.

Determine the "value" of the stock certificates

5. Add the value of all the coins depicted in the border to find the total value of the certificate.
6. In crayon, write that value in large numbers on the certificate.
7. Imagine that the coin value represents the actual value of each stock. Compare stocks. Which is most valuable? Which is least expensive?

Add details to stock certificates

5. Choose an imaginary amount of money to invest in stocks. Research current stock market reports to find the cost of one share of stock for the company portrayed on the stock certificate.
6. Students calculate how many shares they could purchase with the amount of money they chose. Record that information as an equation.
7. Students research who in their chosen corporations might sign the stock certificates. Or students invent names as representatives of the companies. Add detailed text, embellishments, and imaginary signatures to stock certificates.

8. Use glitter glue to add sparkle to certificates. Air-dry.

Process: Session 3 30-45 min.

Identify stock value

9. Form small groups. Write equations to reflect the value of the group's stock. If the group were to sell the stock, what could they buy with its value? Repeat several times.

Track stock values

9. Track the value of the publicly traded stock for at least a month. Graph its daily value.

Analyze investments

9. Track two publicly traded stocks and compare which stock makes more money over the course of at least a month. Make line graphs to show their relative daily values. At the end of the time periods, analyze which one would have been the better investment. What trends are evident?

K-2	3-4	5-6

Assessment

- Are crayon rubbings clear and precise and are border designs enhanced with colorful lines, shapes, and patterns?
- Does the monetary value printed on the certificates equal the total value of the coins pictured in the border designs?
- Do students accurately compare the values of the certificates made by classmates?
- Does text provide information about the company?

- Do border designs show attention to line, shape, color, texture, and pattern?
- Do certificates include the company name, a symbol reflecting the company's product, and signatures of important company leaders, as well as decorative border designs?
- Are students able to read stock market charts, identify values, and compute the number of shares that can be purchased for a given amount of money?
- Students write a short paragraph describing how investments can benefit both stockholders and business.

- Ask students to reflect on this lesson and write a DREAM statement to summarize the most important things they learned.

Extensions

Talk about why companies create ads. Invite students to pretend they have been asked to make up a name for a new product. What are some of their ideas? See the New Names lesson plan on Crayola.com.

Invite a representative from a local bank to talk to the class about the value of saving money. See how to make a Bits and Pieces Bird Bank on Crayola.com.

Introduce students to a stock market game such as *Pit* and provide time for playing.

Ask students who are interested in product research to trace a specific product from its origin to its final destination. Who was involved in product design? What raw materials are used? How, where, and by what company is it manufactured? How was it transported? Consider the Trucks at Work lesson plan found on Crayola.com as an example.

Young children and those with learning differences might benefit from a hands-on business project such as a class booth at a school carnival to sell bookmarks, gift bags, or other craft projects. Ask families to "invest" quarters. Children determine how many raw materials can be purchased for the amount invested and how much they will charge for the products. How will the business be promoted? How many sales staff are needed at what times? Students keep track of sales and add up total income. How will they divide the money among investors? Will everyone get back their original investment? Will they make a profit?

New York Stock Exchange
Certificate of Listing
Binney & Smith Inc.

Crayola **Dream~Makers**
Building fun and creativity into standards-based learning

Geometric Weaving

Objectives

Students (K-2) observe and duplicate patterns, relations, and functions of two-dimensional design in weaving.

Students (3-4) investigate and note how a change in one variable relates to a change in a second variable as it applies to parallel and perpendicular lines and two-dimensional congruent figures in weaving.

Students (5-6) represent, analyze, and generalize a variety of weaving patterns as they work in pairs to create paper weavings with balanced designs.

Multiple Intelligences

Bodily-kinesthetic
Interpersonal
Logical-mathematical
Spatial

What Does It Mean?

Warp: the threads that run lengthwise on a loom

Weft: the threads that are woven over and under the warp threads

National Standards

Visual Arts Standard #6	Mathematics Standards
Makes connections between visual arts and other disciplines	**Geometry** Specify locations and describe spatial relationships using coordinate geometry and other representational systems **Algebra** Understand patterns, relations, and functions

Background Information

Weaving, embroidery, and appliqué have long been vital elements of African artistry. The Kuba who live in the Kasai river region of the Democratic Republic of Congo are known for their beautiful raffia cloth weavings.

Kuba cloth is woven from the fiber of the *raphia vinifera* palm. Production of these textiles is a multiple-stage process, involving the men, women, and children of a clan. The process includes gathering and preparing the raffia fibers, weaving the cloth, dyeing the embroidery fibers, and embellishing the cloth with embroidery, appliqué, patchwork, and dye.

Historically, Kuba cloths have been buried with kings or those fortunate enough to own them as a sign of status. The geometric patterns also have inspired modern artists such as Picasso and Klee. Today these cloths are traded to surrounding areas and are occasionally used for ceremonial dress and to cover royal stools.

Resources

Abuela's Weave by Omar S. Castaneda
All ages. Story of a Guatemalan weaver and her granddaughter. Contrasts the value of hand weaving with mass-manufactured tapestries.

Kuba by Rebecca Luechak
Details about the society, history, and art of the Kuba people of central Africa. Color illustrations appeal to students of all ages.

Master Weaver From Ghana by Gilbert Ahiagble and Louise Meyer
For older students. Visit a West African family and community where the kente cloth weaving trade is a group effort.

Vocabulary List

Use this list to explore new vocabulary, create idea webs, or brainstorm related subjects.

- Math terms

Angle	Perpendicular
Axis	Quadrant
Balance	Right angle
Congruent	Shape
Line	X-axis
Parallel	Y-axis

- Art terms

Design	Warp
Mirror	Weaving
Tandem	Weft
Texture	

Artwork by students from
Gayman Elementary School,
Plumstead, Pennsylvania.
Teacher: Cara Lucente

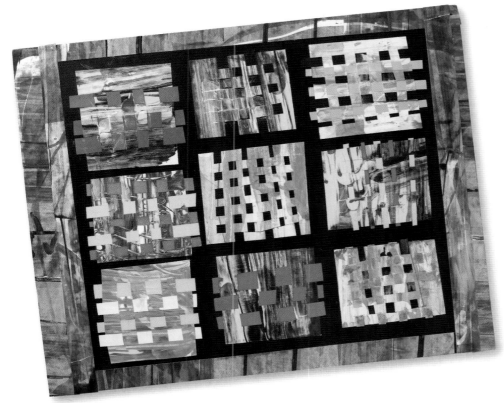

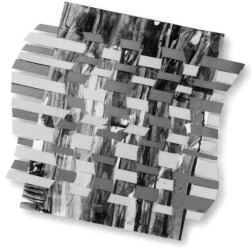

Artwork by students from
Jordan Community School,
Chicago, Illinois.
Teacher: Elyse Martin

	K-2	3-4	5-6
Suggested Preparation and Discussion	Show examples of pairs of lines that are parallel and pairs of lines that are perpendicular. Ask each student to use colored pencils to demonstrate their understanding of these concepts.	Introduce/review the geometric concept of perpendicular and parallel lines. Ask students to use math terminology to describe the angle formed by two perpendicular lines. Observe that at the intersection of two perpendicular lines, there is a 90° angle, like the corner of a square.	
		Explore the algebraic concept of number lines. Ask students where they have seen lines like these (maps, graphs). Introduce the concept of using coordinates to plan points and shapes in a design using a number grid to indicate the placement of lines, corners, and other features.	Review/introduce basic algebraic concepts. Discuss the use of an axis as a line used to locate points. Introduce the concept of a perpendicular axis used to locate points in a two-dimensional space or plane. Draw an x –axis and y-axis on a grid to demonstrate how points can be placed in each quadrant. Demonstrate how points are named and how to balance points on opposing sides of each axis. Draw simple shapes using points in each quadrant.
	Introduce the concept of mirror images. Have students share examples. Draw a vertical line on a white board. Ask one student to draw a large dot (point) on the left side of the line. Ask another student to draw the mirror image of that point on the other side of the line. Continue this activity with lines and shapes to practice creating a balanced design. Repeat with a horizontal line. Older students might repeat the activity with both horizontal and vertical lines at the same time, intersecting perpendicularly.		

Display samples of weaving, both actual and in photographs. Introduce terms such as line and shape, warp and weft, and over and under as students look at the samples. Draw attention to samples where the weaving lines (warps and wefts) are perpendicular to each other.

Provide paper for students to create small, simple tabby weavings. Use art and math terminology to describe the weaving process and result.

Create a paper weaving that illustrates a simple tabby weave—over and under with a warp and weft.

Geometric Weaving

	K-2	3-4	5-6
Crayola® Supplies	• Colored Pencils • Glitter Glue • School Glue • Scissors • Washable Markers		
		• Paint Brushes	
Other Materials	• Brown grocery bags • Craft paper roll • Rulers • White drawing paper		
		• Paper towels • Recycled newspaper • Water containers	
Set-up/Tips		• Cover art area with newspaper.	
Process: Session 1 20-30 min.	**Design paper** 1. Decorate two papers with lines, colors, shapes, and patterns using washable markers.	**Design patterned paper** 1. Decorate two papers with patterns using washable markers and colored pencils. 2. Use wet brushes on marker designs for a watercolor effect. Air-dry.	**Design complex patterns on paper** 1. Challenge student pairs to create complex designs on two papers by drawing shapes. 2. Fill in shapes with solid colors or patterns so they mirror each other.
Process: Session 2 20-30 min.	**Cut one design sheet into weft strips** 3. Use a ruler and colored pencils to measure, mark, and cut strips of paper from **one** of the decorated sheets. Measure strips as follows: K-2: 1-inch strips Grades 3-4: 3/4-inch strips Grades 5-6: Graduate the width of the strips so that each measures 1/2 inch at one end and a full inch at the other 4. Add glitter glue to the warp sheet and weft strips. Air-dry glue.		
Process: Session 3 30-40 min.	**Create the warp strips and weave** 5. Show students how to fold down an inch at the top of the second decorated sheet. Demonstrate how to measure and mark lines to create warp strips. Students in K to 2 measure 1-inch vertical strips. Students in grades 3 to 6 measure 1/2-inch vertical strips. (Grades 5-6 do NOT graduate width of warp strips.) Cut along drawn lines to create strips, stopping at the top fold, so the strips remain connected. 6. With a partner, create a simple tabby weave by weaving each weft strip over and under the warp strips. Tightly tuck the first strip under the top fold.		
			7. Show students how to alternate which end of the weft strip leads through the warp so that the graduated widths compliment each other. Demonstrate what happens if they are not alternated. 8. For added effects, cut thinner strips of colored paper and interweave them over and under the tabby weave pattern.
	8. Alternate the over-under pattern with each weft. Tightly tuck all strips close to the previous weft until all strips are used.		
Process: Session 4 30-40 min.	**Secure weavings to backings** 9. Cut apart brown paper grocery bags and spread flat. Glue weavings to the plain sides of the bags so they do not unravel. 10. Glue all weavings together on craft paper to create a mural reflecting African Kuba textiles.		

	K-2	3-4	5-6
Assessment	• Check that students included line, shape, color, and pattern in their paper designs. • Students successfully complete the simple tabby weave process.	• Students achieved a watercolor effect with their designs. • Students successfully weave their strips.	• Talk with partners as they work. Assess use of proper math and art terminology as students describe what they are drawing. Reinforce learning by using proper terminology in response to their comments. Check accuracy of designs created by partners. • Observe cooperative efforts to measure and weave in pairs.

• Display and discuss finished weavings. Assess use of proper terminology as students offer observations on each other's work.

• Ask students to reflect on this lesson and write a DREAM statement to summarize the most important things they learned.

Extensions			
	Introduce children to wiggly weaving. See Crayola.com for a Wiggly Weaving craft idea for inspiration. Create and use number lines when reading stories with students to begin to formulate the concept of x-axis as a progression of value or (in stories) of time. Students add illustrations to class timelines to demonstrate events occurring over time.	Challenge students to design weaving sheets that demonstrate mirror images using all four quadrants of an x- and y-axis. Measure, rule out, and cut weft strips of their designs. Create a twill weave, with weft strips going over two warps and then under one or two warps. See the Rainbow in a Rug lesson plan on Crayola.com to create a replica of Navajo weaving. Make Fiesta Mats for a Mexican culture celebration and create West African kente cloth with Crayola Overwriters®.	Show students how to plot ordered pairs on the coordinate plane of a paper weaving. Create paper weavings using equal-width, straight strips. Draw a four-quadrant x- and y-axis on the weaving and number each line (+ going up and to the right, - going down and to the left). Model how to plot (x, y) coordinates. Plot coordinates as simple points or small shapes and symbols on their weavings.
	Young children and students whose manual dexterity is not fully developed may have better success working with lightweight poster board rather than drawing paper. Provide help with cutting if necessary.	Encourage gifted students to find out more about weavings created by other cultures and report their findings to the class. Some might also enjoy researching artists who have created the illusion of weaving in their paintings such as Paul Klee, Piet Mondrian, and Picasso.	

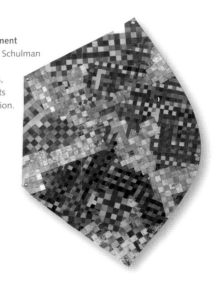

Rapid I Movement
Artist: Barbara Schulman
33" x 23"
Acrylic, canvas, brass grommets
Private Collection.

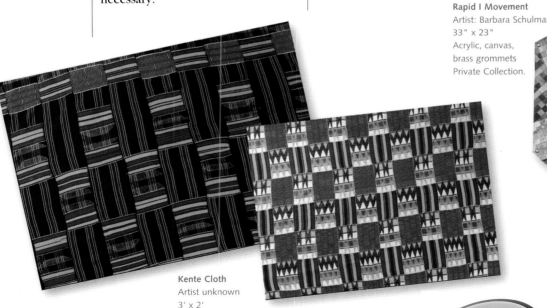

Kente Cloth
Artist unknown
3' x 2'
Dyed cotton
Private Collection.

The lessons in this guide suggest types of art materials. This chart outlines the specific characteristics of different Crayola art materials. Use it to choose which variation best meets your needs and those of your students. Crayola products are subject to change. Check Crayola.com for the most recent information.

CRAYONS/OIL PASTELS	CHARACTERISTICS
Regular Crayons (3-5/8" x 5/16")	• Brilliant colors; smooth, even color lay down.
Large Size Crayons (4" x 7/16")	• Brilliant colors; smooth, even color lay down. • Larger size for younger child palm grip.
Triangular Crayons	• Brilliant colors; smooth, even color lay down. • Triangular shape helps guide correct pincer grip. • Anti-roll.
Washable Crayons	• Brilliant colors; smooth, even color lay down. • Available in regular, large, and triangular sizes. • Superior washability from walls, tables, and most surfaces.
Construction Paper™ Crayons	• Brilliant colors; smooth, even color lay down. • Color shows on dark paper, brown craft paper, and similar surfaces.
Fabric Crayons	• Permanent when drawing is heat transferred to synthetic fabric.
Twistables® Crayons	• Brilliant colors; smooth, even color lay down. • Durable plastic barrel. • No sharpening with easy twist-up action.
Twistables Erasable Crayons	• Complete erasability of marks. • Brilliant colors; smooth, even color lay down. • Durable plastic barrel. • No sharpening with easy twist-up action. • Eraser on each crayon.
Twistables Slick Stix™ Crayons	• Super-smooth color glides on paper. • Water soluble upon application. • Dries quickly with no smearing. • Durable plastic barrel. • Great for older student crayon techniques. • Appropriate for students with special needs due to ease of color lay down.
Oil Pastels	• Opaque colors blend easily. • Good color lay down. • Hexagonal shape prevents rolling.
Portfolio® Series Oil Pastels	• Opaque colors blend and layer well, with velvety lay down. • Unique water solubility allows watercolor washes.

MARKERS	CHARACTERISTICS
Regular Markers	• Bright, brilliant, transparent colors. • Conical tip draws thick and thin lines. • Fine tip draws thin lines and detail.
Washable Markers	• Washability you can trust™–superior washability from hands and most clothing. • Bright, brilliant, transparent colors. • Conical tip draws thick and thin lines. • Fine tip draws thin lines and detail. • Wedge tip provides ease in broad strokes and vertical applications.
Gel Markers	• Bright, opaque colors that deliver bold marks on black and dark papers. • World's most washable marker with superior washability from hands and most clothing. • Writes on glass, foil, glossy, and other non-porous surfaces. • Conical tip draws thick and thin lines.
Overwriters® Markers	• Bright "overcolors" magically color over darker "undercolors" for exciting and dramatic effects.
Color Changeables™ Markers	• Students have fun seeing colors magically "pop out" over each other for new creative expression possibilities. • Increased color variety as "wand" changes 7 colors to 7 new colors.
Twistables Markers	• No lost caps! • Bright, brilliant, transparent colors.
Fabric Markers	• Permanent bright color on cotton or cotton blends when heat set. • Bullet tip for medium and fine detail.
Dry-Erase Markers	• Low odor, bold color that can be viewed from a distance. • Chisel and bullet tips.

COLORED PENCILS	CHARACTERISTICS
Colored Pencils	• Bright, vivid colors with opaque lay down. • Good blending. • Thick 3 mm colored cores; made from reforested wood.
Watercolor Colored Pencils	• Water soluble for watercolor and drawing effects. • Bright, vivid colors with opaque lay down. • Good blending. • Thick 3 mm colored cores; made from reforested wood.
Erasable Colored Pencils	• Complete erasability of pencil marks. • Bright colors with opaque lay down. • Good blending. • Eraser on each pencil. • Thick 3 mm colored cores; made from reforested wood.
Twistables Colored Pencils	• Bright colors; smooth, even color lay down. • Durable plastic barrel. • No sharpening with easy twist-up action.
Twistables Erasable Colored Pencils	• Complete erasability of pencil marks. • Bright colors; smooth, even color lay down. • Durable plastic barrel. • No sharpening with easy twist-up action. • Eraser on each pencil.
Write Start® Colored Pencils	• Thick 5.3 mm colored cores and large hexagonal barrels are great for young students. • Bright, vivid colors with opaque lay down. • Anti-roll. • Made from reforested wood.

MODELING COMPOUNDS	CHARACTERISTICS
Air-Dry Clay	• No firing, air-dry clay. • Good for high-detail projects. • Natural clay body to create solid, durable forms. • Suitable for all clay techniques. • White color suitable for all color/surface decoration. • Air-dries hard.
Model Magic®	• Soft, easy-to-manipulate compound. • Good for low-detail projects. • Good for young students and those who are developing manual dexterity. • Air-dries to consistency of a foam cup.
Modeling Clay	• Traditional oil-based clay. • Non-hardening and reusable.

PAINTS	CHARACTERISTICS
Premier™ Tempera	• Ultimate opacity and coverage. • Creamy consistency flows smoothly and will not crack or flake. • Intense, true hues for accurate color mixing.
Artista II® value-priced Tempera	• Fine-quality colors with good opacity. • Creamy consistency flows smoothly and will not crack or flake. • Good hues for excellent color mixtures. • Washable from skin and fabrics.
Washable Paint	• Washability you can trust–superior washability from skin and fabrics. • Bright, clean colors for consistent color mixing. • Smooth-flowing formula will not crack or flake.
Acrylic Paint	• Pigment-rich colors are intense even when diluted; achieve accurate color mixes. • Thick, tube-like viscosity, for a variety of techniques from air-brushing to impasto. • Permanent, water resistant, and flexible when dry.
Washable Finger Paint	• Bright colors, thick consistency. • Washable from skin and fabrics.
Watercolors	• Bright, intense, transparent colors. • True hues for accurate color mixing. • Ideal for opaque and transparent techniques.
Washable Watercolors	• Washability you can trust–superior washability from skin and fabrics. • Bright, intense, transparent colors.